GAPS Family Cookbook

100 Recipes to Nourish the Whole Family

ANDRE PARKER

"Andre has done a fine job of putting together some delicious looking GAPS recipes. These recipes can be used as a quick entry into the GAPS Protocol, guiding the person as their body recommends. GAPS is not easy, especially when it involves a whole new way of cooking. Learning recipes that are already laid out can ease the transition."

Becky Plotner, ND, traditional naturopath, CGP, D.PSc.
"The GAPS Expert" according to Dr. Natasha Campbell-McBride

Table of Contents

Introduction

This book was created with the intention of not only helping you support your own digestive health by implementing GAPS-friendly recipes into your diet but also by including recipes your entire family will love as well. Starting a GAPS diet can be one of the most rewarding things you can do for your health, and getting the whole family involved will not only make meal preparation easier and less time-consuming, but it will also mean more support as you go on your own GAPS journey.

Before we jump into why I decided to create a family-style GAPS recipe book, I want to touch upon what the GAPS diet is.

What is the GAPS Diet?

The GAPS Diet was developed by Dr. Natasha Campbell-McBride MD. It stands for Gut and Psychology Syndrome and was derived from the Specific Carbohydrate Diet to help treat inflammatory conditions of the digestive tract. Dr. Natasha Campbell-McBride developed this diet as a way to help her patients suffering from different digestive, as well as neurological, conditions, thought to have been caused by an imbalance in the bacteria in the gut. This is where the idea for the GAPS diet came about. Dr. Campbell-McBride developed this protocol to help create a process for removing foods that are hard to digest and then adding in nutrient-dense foods that can help support gut healing. As you follow a GAPS diet, you will go through different stages from the introduction stage all the way up to the Full GAPS Diet. As your body allows you to progress, you will be able to add more and more nutrient-dense foods into your diet.

So, who is the GAPS diet for? The GAPS diet can be beneficial for those with digestive health issues, but also those who suffer from ADHD, anxiety, depression and autoimmune disease as these are all things that link back to the health of the digestive system.

Why a Family GAPS Recipe Book?

I wanted to create a recipe book keeping family in mind as I know first-hand how powerful and effective the GAPS diet can be. This was the diet that radically changed my health, and I wanted to share my belief in the GAPS diet by creating recipes for the whole family as gut health is just as important for the little ones in the family as well. I wanted to create recipes that could be adapted to be kid-friendly to help get kids off to a good start. To make sure each recipe created in this book was completely GAPS-compliant, the recipes have been reviewed by Becky Plotner, ND, Traditional Naturopath, CGP, D. PSc also known as "The GAPS Expert" according to Dr. Natasha Campbell-McBride.

In this book, you will find notes on how to make each recipe baby-friendly, tips on making the recipes suitable for a lunch or picnic to take with you on family outings and some useful storage tips.

I hope that you find this book resourceful and that you are able to take these recipes and create delicious and nourishing meals for your entire family to enjoy. There is no better way to support one another than by taking a stand to safeguard your health and to teach your kids and loved ones the importance of taking care of your health through the foods that you eat.

How to Use This Book

Before you get started, I want to take a minute to stress the importance of working with a Certified Practitioner while following a GAPS diet and continuing to work with your health care practitioner throughout your GAPS journey as well.

This book should not be used as a how-to-heal guide, but rather a resource for GAPS recipes. If you are looking for more detail and a more in-depth analysis of the GAPS Diet, I encourage you to read Dr. Natasha Campbell-McBride's GAPS book and to continue to work with your health care practitioners to get you feeling your best.

STAGE 1

Chicken Stock

Serves: 10
Prep Time: 10 minutes
Cook Time: Just over 2 hours

Ingredients:

- 2 lbs. of chicken pieces (legs, wings, necks)
- 2 quarts of filtered water
- 2 carrots, chopped
- 6 cloves of garlic, chopped
- 2 sprigs of fresh rosemary
- 5 sprigs of fresh thyme
- 5 sprigs of fresh parsley
- 1 bay leaf
- 3/4 Tbsp. mineral salt
- 1 Tbsp. black peppercorns (crushed and cooked in a cache that can be removed)

Directions:

1. Add the chicken parts to the pan with water to cover the pieces.
2. Add the minerals salt, and springs.
3. Bring to a boil, and then scoop off the foam from the top as it starts to boil. By the time you're done fully scooping off the foam and discarding, it should be at a complete boil.
4. Turn the pot to a low simmer to where the pot has an occasional bubble.
5. Put a lid on and let it cook for two hours.
6. The skin and connective tissues, if soft, can be added back in and blended into the soup.
7. After it is cooked and stored in mason jars, it can be cooked for another 20-30 minutes with vegetables prior to eating.
8. Freeze any leftover stock to have on hand when you need homemade stock and are short on time.

Pumpkin Bowl

Serves: 4
Prep time: 5 minutes
Cook time: 30 minutes

Ingredients:

- 1 lb. pumpkin, peeled, seeds removed and cubed
- 1 Tbsp. coconut oil
- 1 pinch mineral salt
- 1 Tbsp. raw honey
- Homemade meat stock for cooking

Directions:

1. Fill a pot with meat stock, and add the pumpkin.
2. Cover and bring to a simmer. Cook in the stock for 30 minutes, or until the pumpkin is very soft.
3. Scoop out the pumpkin, and set aside the stock to use with something else. Add the coconut oil and salt to the pumpkin, and use a fork to mash it up. Stir in the honey and enjoy.

Storage: Store any leftover pumpkin in an airtight container in the fridge for up to 5 days.

Baby Food: Omit the honey and salt.

Zucchini Mint Soup

Serves: 4
Prep time: 5 minutes
Cook time: 30 minutes

Ingredients:

- 4 cups homemade meat stock
- 2 cups water
- 2 cloves garlic
- ½ tsp. mineral salt
- 1 Tbsp. coconut oil
- 2 large zucchinis, chopped
- 1 cup cauliflower florets
- 1 large stem fresh mint (keep intact)

Directions:

1. In a large pot, add the stock, water, garlic, salt, coconut oil, zucchinis and cauliflower. Add the mint in a cache and add to the pot. If everything is not completely covered, add more stock or water.
2. Bring to a boil, then reduce the heat to low and simmer for 30 minutes, or until the vegetables are cooked through.
3. Remove the mint from the soup, then purée until smooth.

Storage: Store any leftovers in an airtight container in the fridge for up to 5 days or in the freezer for up to a month.

Baby Food: Omit the salt from the recipe or add the salt after removing a portion for the baby. If you want to make it thicker, add extra zucchini and cauliflower to the baby's portion before blending it separately.

Lunchbox/Picnic: This soup is also great cold, so bring it on a picnic or pack it in a lunchbox with an ice pack.

Creamed Cauliflower with Beef

Serves: 4
Prep time: 10 minutes
Cook time: 30 minutes

Ingredients:

- 4 cups homemade meat stock
- 1 head cauliflower, cut into florets
- 2 cloves garlic
- 1 Tbsp. coconut oil
- ½ tsp. mineral salt
- 1 lb. organic grass-fed beef stew meat, cooked and cut into bite-sized cubes (must be cooked in meat stock for this stage)
- Homemade sauerkraut juice as tolerated

Directions:

1. In a large pot, add the stock, cauliflower, garlic, coconut oil and salt. Bring to a boil, then reduce the heat to low and simmer for 30 minutes, or until the cauliflower is very soft.
2. Transfer the contents in the pot to a blender and blend until smooth. It should be runny but still quite thick. Return the mixture to the pot.
3. Add the cooked beef and mineral salt.
4. Serve with homemade sauerkraut juice as tolerated.

Storage: Store any leftovers in an airtight container in the fridge for up to 3-4 days.

Baby Food: Omit the salt from the cauliflower purée.

Chicken Zoodle Soup

Serves: 4
Prep time: 10 minutes
Cook time: 35 minutes

Ingredients:

- 4 cups homemade meat stock
- 2 cloves garlic
- ½ tsp. mineral salt
- 2 large carrots, cut into ribbons
- 1 large zucchini, cut into ribbons
- 1 lb. cooked organic pasture-raised chicken thighs (these must be cooked in meat stock for this stage)
- Homemade sauerkraut juice as tolerated

Directions:

1. In a large pot, add the stock, garlic, salt, carrot ribbons and zucchini ribbons. If everything is not completely covered, add more stock or water.
2. Bring to a boil, then reduce the heat to low and simmer for 30 minutes.
3. Add the cooked chicken meat to the soup and heat for another 5 minutes.
4. Serve with homemade sauerkraut juice as tolerated.

Storage: Store any leftovers in an airtight container in the fridge for up to 3-4 days or in the freezer for up to a month.

Baby Food: Boil extra zucchini and carrots in a salt-free, homemade meat stock and purée.

Lunchbox/Picnic: Store the soup in an insulated lunchbox or cooler with an ice pack.

Asian Chicken and Broccoli Soup

Serves: 4
Prep time: 10 minutes
Cook time: 10 minutes

Ingredients:

- 4 cups homemade meat stock
- 2 cups filtered water
- 1 onion, sliced
- 1 clove garlic
- 2-inch piece of fresh ginger (in a cache)
- ½ tsp. mineral salt
- 3 cups broccoli florets
- 1 lb. organic pasture-raised chicken thighs, cooked (must be cooked in meat stock for this stage)
- Homemade sauerkraut juice

Directions:

1. In a large pot, add the stock, water, onion, garlic, salt and broccoli.
2. Add the ginger in a cache to the pot.
3. Bring to a boil, then reduce the heat to low and simmer for 10 minutes. Remove the ginger, add in the cooked chicken and stir.
4. Serve with sauerkraut juice as tolerated.

Storage: Store any leftovers in an airtight container in the fridge for up to 3-4 days or in the freezer for up to a month.

Baby Food: Add the salt to the recipe once you have set aside a portion for the baby. Alternatively, set aside extra broccoli and stock to cook separately and purée until smooth or serve as finger food if doing baby-led weaning.

Can't Beet Pumpkin Soup

Serves: 4
Prep time: 10 minutes
Cook time: 30 minutes

Ingredients:

- 6 cups homemade meat stock
- 1 onion, sliced
- 1 clove garlic
- 2-inch piece fresh ginger (in a cache)
- ½ tsp. mineral salt
- 2 cups fresh pumpkin, cubed (skin and seeds removed)
- 1 large beet, cubed
- Homemade sauerkraut juice as tolerated.

Directions:

1. In a large pot, add the stock, onion, garlic, salt, pumpkin and beet.
2. Add the ginger in a cache to the pot.
3. Bring to a boil, then reduce the heat to low and simmer for 30 minutes, or until cooked through.
4. Remove the ginger.
5. Serve with sauerkraut juice as tolerated.

Storage: Store any leftovers in an airtight container in the fridge for up to 5 days or in the freezer for up to a month.

Baby Food: Set aside extra squash, beets and stock to cook in the same way in a separate pan and purée until smooth.

Lunchbox/Picnic: This soup is great cold. Pack in an insulated lunch box/cooler with an ice pack.

Carrot Leek Soup

Serves: 4
Prep time: 5 minutes
Cook time: 30 minutes

Ingredients:

- 6 cups homemade meat stock
- 2 cloves garlic
- 1 tsp. mineral salt
- 1 onion, chopped
- ¼ cup leek, chopped
- 4 large carrots, chopped
- 1 large sprig fresh rosemary (keep intact)
- Homemade sauerkraut juice as tolerated

Directions:

1. In a large pot over high heat, add the stock, garlic and salt. Bring to a boil, then reduce the heat to low. Add the onion, leek, carrots and rosemary. If everything is not completely covered, add more stock or water.
2. Simmer for 30 minutes, or until the vegetables are cooked through.
3. Remove the rosemary from the soup, then purée until smooth.
4. Serve with sauerkraut juice. Enjoy however much is tolerated.

Storage: Store any leftovers in an airtight container in the fridge for up to 5 days or in the freezer for up to a month.

Baby Food: This soup is great for babies if you omit the salt and serve it lukewarm or cold.

Lunchbox/Picnic: This soup is great cold. Pack it in an insulated lunch box/cooler with an ice pack.

STAGE 2

Pumpkin with Raw Honey and Sea Salt

Serves: 4
Prep time: 10 minutes
Cook time: 10-15 minutes

Ingredients:

- 1 lb. pumpkin, peeled, seeded and cut into bite-sized cubes
- 2 cups meat stock
- 1 Tbsp. raw honey
- 1 Tbsp. coconut oil, melted
- ¼ tsp. mineral salt

Directions:

1. Fill a large pot over a medium heat with the meat stock. Add the pumpkin and simmer for 10-15 minutes or until the pumpkin is soft.
2. Remove from the pot and drizzle with honey and coconut oil, and then sprinkle with salt.

Storage: Store any leftover pumpkin in the fridge for up to 5 days.

Baby Food: Omit the salt and honey from the baby's portion.

Lunchbox/Picnic: This is a great packable snack for a lunchbox or picnic. No need for ice!

Breakfast Egg Drop Soup

Serves: 4
Prep time: 5 minutes
Cook time: 15 minutes

Ingredients:

- 4 cups homemade meat stock
- ½ cup onion, chopped
- 1 sprig fresh rosemary
- ¼ tsp. mineral salt
- 4 organic pasture-raised egg yolks

Directions:

1. Add the stock, onion, rosemary and salt to a pot. Simmer for 15 minutes or until the onion is softened.
2. Remove the rosemary sprig. Divide into equal portions and add an egg yolk into each soup.

Storage: Store any leftovers in an airtight container in the fridge for up to 3-4 days or in the freezer for up to a month.

Baby Food: A cup of homemade stock without the salt or the egg yolk stirred in is great for babies. Serve lukewarm or cold in a sippy cup.

Chicken and Squash Casserole

Serves: 4
Prep time: 5 minutes
Cook time: 30 minutes

Ingredients:

- 2 Tbsp. homemade ghee
- 1 cup homemade meat stock
- 1 onion, chopped
- 1 lb. summer squash, peeled, seeds removed and cubed
- 1 lb. organic pasture-raised chicken thighs
- ½ tsp. mineral salt

Directions:

1. Preheat the oven to 375°F.
2. In a casserole dish, add the ghee, stock, onion and squash. Nestle the chicken thighs into the vegetables and sprinkle with salt.
3. Bake in the oven for 30 minutes or until the squash and chicken are cooked through.

Storage: Store any leftovers in an airtight container in the fridge for 3-4 days or in the freezer for up to a month.

Note: With any stage two recipe that is cooked in the oven, it is important to remove the crunchy part of the final cooked recipe on top and only eat the soft middle and bottom portions. You can look forward to enjoying the entire recipe, with the crunchy parts, in stage four!

Baby Food: Cook extra squash on the stove in salt-free, homemade stock and purée until smooth.

Lemon Chicken and Green Bean Soup

Serves: 4
Prep time: 10 minutes
Cook time: 20 minutes

Ingredients:

- 2 Tbsp. homemade ghee
- 1 onion, chopped
- ½ tsp. mineral salt
- 4 cups homemade chicken meat stock
- 1 lb. organic pasture-raised chicken thighs, cooked (you can use the meat from the chicken used to make the homemade meat stock)
- 2 cups green beans, chopped
- 1 clove garlic, crushed
- 4 organic pasture-raised egg yolks

Directions:

1. In a large pot, warm the ghee over a medium to low heat. Add the onion and salt and cook for 5 minutes, until the onions are soft but not brown.
2. Add the stock, green beans and garlic. Bring to a boil, then reduce the heat, cover and simmer for 15 minutes.
3. Add the cooked chicken to the soup and stir.
4. Enjoy each serving with an egg yolk stirred into your soup while hot.

Storage: Store any leftover soup in an airtight container in the fridge for up to 3-4 days or in the freezer for up to a month.

Baby Food: Cook extra green beans and onions separately and purée with homemade meat stock.

Root Vegetable and Beef Casserole

Serves: 4
Prep time: 5 minutes
Cook time: 45 minutes

Ingredients:

- 2 Tbsp. homemade ghee
- 3 cups homemade meat stock
- 1 onion, chopped
- 1 large beet, chopped
- 2 turnips, chopped
- 1 lb. organic grass-fed ground beef
- 2 sprigs fresh rosemary
- ½ tsp. mineral salt
- Homemade sauerkraut juice as tolerated.

Directions:

1. Preheat the oven to 350°F.
2. In a casserole dish, add the ghee, stock, onion, beet, turnips and rosemary. Nestle chunks of ground beef into the vegetables and sprinkle with salt.
3. Bake in the oven for 45 minutes or until the vegetables and beef are cooked through.
4. Remove from the oven and remove the fresh rosemary sprigs.
5. Stir in the sauerkraut juice. Add as much as tolerated.

Note: With any stage two recipe that is cooked in the oven, it is important to remove the crunchy part of the final cooked recipe on top and only eat the soft middle and bottom portions. You can look forward to enjoying the entire recipe, with the crunchy parts, in stage four!

Storage: Store any leftovers in an airtight container in the fridge for up to 3-4 days or in the freezer for up to a month.

Baby Food: Cook extra root vegetables on the stove in salt-free, homemade meat stock and purée until smooth or serve as finger food if doing baby-led weaning.

Beefy Leafy Green Casserole

Serves: 4
Prep time: 15 minutes
Cook time: 45 minutes

Ingredients:

- 1 onion, chopped
- 1 clove garlic, chopped
- 2 cups spinach
- 3 cups kale, chopped with the fibrous stem removed
- 2 cups homemade meat stock
- 1 lb. organic grass-fed ground beef
- 2 Tbsp. homemade ghee, melted
- 1 tsp. mineral salt
- 4 organic pasture-raised egg yolks

Directions:

1. Preheat the oven to 350°F.
2. Add the onion, garlic, spinach and kale to the baking dish. Pour the stock on top.
3. In a bowl, mix together the ground beef, ghee and salt. Place in chunks on top of the greens.
4. Bake in the oven for about 45 minutes or until the beef is cooked through.
5. Serve topped with the egg yolks.

Storage: Store any leftovers in an airtight container in the fridge for up to 3-4 days.

Note: With any stage two recipe that is cooked in the oven, it is important to remove the crunchy part of the final cooked recipe on top and only eat the soft middle and bottom portions. You can look forward to enjoying the entire recipe, with the crunchy parts, in stage four!

Baby Food: Cook extra leafy greens, along with any other vegetables on hand, in a pot on the stove with salt-free, homemade stock. Purée until smooth.

Cauliflower and Ground Beef Mash

Serves: 4
Prep time: 10 minutes
Cook time: 45 minutes

Ingredients:

- 1 lb. organic grass-fed ground beef
- 1 onion, chopped
- 2 cloves garlic, chopped
- 1 tsp. mineral salt, divided
- 4 cups cauliflower florets
- 2 Tbsp. homemade ghee, melted
- 1 cup homemade meat stock
- 4 organic pasture-raised egg yolks

Directions:

1. Preheat the oven to 350°F.
2. In a bowl, mix together the beef, garlic, onion and half a teaspoon of salt.
3. In a casserole dish, add the cauliflower and toss with the melted ghee and the remaining half teaspoon of salt.
4. Scoop the ground beef on top of the cauliflower, then pour the stock over the top and bake in the oven for 45 minutes, or until the cauliflower and beef are cooked through.
5. Remove from the oven, take off the top layer and use a potato masher to mash everything else up.
6. Serve topped with the egg yolks.

Storage: Store any leftovers in an airtight container in the fridge for up to 3-4 days.

Note: With any stage 2 recipe that is cooked in the oven, it is important to remove the crunchy part of the final cooked recipe on top and only eat the soft middle and bottom portions. You can look forward to enjoying the entire recipe, with the crunchy parts, in stage four!

Baby Food: Cook extra cauliflower, along with any other vegetables on hand, in a pot on the stove with salt-free, homemade stock. Purée until smooth.

STAGE 3

Pumpkin Almond Pancakes

Serves: 2
Prep time: 10 minutes
Cook time: 5 minutes

Ingredients:

- ½ cup pumpkin, peeled, seeded, steamed and mashed
- 3 Tbsp. almond butter (homemade)
- 2 organic pasture-raised eggs
- ¼ tsp. mineral salt
- 3 Tbsp. homemade ghee

Directions:

1. In a bowl, mix together the pumpkin, almond butter, eggs and salt.
2. In a large skillet, melt the ghee over a medium to low heat. Scoop half the batter into the pan to form small pancakes.
3. Cook for about 2-3 minutes per side, being careful not to let it burn.
4. Repeat the above with the rest of the batter.
5. Enjoy warm, topped with more ghee, if desired.

Storage: Store any leftovers in an airtight container in the fridge for up to 2-3 days.

Baby Food: Cut the pancakes into thin strips as finger food.

Lunchbox/Picnic: Pack these pancakes for a perfect snack with lunch or pick-me-up.

Green Egg Scramble

Serves: 2
Prep time: 10 minutes
Cook time: 20-30 minutes

Ingredients:

- 4 organic pasture-raised eggs
- ¼ tsp. mineral salt
- 4 Tbsp. homemade ghee
- 1 small onion, sliced
- 2 cups spinach, chopped
- Sauerkraut as tolerated.

Directions:

1. In a small bowl, whisk together the eggs and salt.
2. In a stockpot, melt the ghee over a low to medium heat, and add the onions and spinach. Cover with a lid and cook for 20-30 minutes, or until the onions are soft and translucent and the spinach is wilted.
3. Add the egg mixture to the stockpot and scramble until cooked through.
4. Enjoy with a side of sauerkraut. Enjoy however much is tolerated.

Storage: Store any leftovers in an airtight container in the fridge for up to 3 days.

Baby Food: Omit the salt for your baby.

Pumpkin Pie Smoothie

Serves: 1
Prep time: 10 minutes
Cook time: 0 minutes

Ingredients:

- ½ cup pumpkin, peeled, seeded, cooked and mashed
- 1 cup filtered water
- 2 Tbsp. homemade yogurt (if tolerated)
- 1 Tbsp. raw honey
- 1 Tbsp. almond butter (homemade)

Directions:

1. Add all of the ingredients to a blender and blend until smooth.
2. Enjoy immediately or store it in the fridge.

Storage: Store any leftovers in an airtight container in the fridge for up to 2 days. Shake or re-blend just before consumption.

Baby Food: Omit the honey and almond butter and purée until smooth.

Poached Salmon and Asparagus

Serves: 4
Prep time: 5 minutes
Cook time: 30-32 minutes

Ingredients:

- 4 cups homemade meat stock
- 1 lb. wild-caught salmon
- 4 Tbsp. homemade ghee plus extra (for serving)
- ½ tsp. mineral salt
- 1 bunch asparagus, trimmed
- ½ avocado, mashed

Directions:

1. In a large pot, bring the stock to a boil. Add the salmon to the pot and simmer for about 10-12 minutes, or until the salmon is cooked through.
2. Remove the salmon from the pot and transfer to a platter. Top with small dollops of ghee and sprinkle with the salt.
3. Next, heat a stockpot over a medium heat with the 4 tablespoons of ghee and add the asparagus. Cover with a lid and cook for 20 minutes or until soft.
4. Serve the asparagus with the salmon and top with the avocado.

Storage: Store any leftovers in an airtight container in the fridge for up to 2 days.

Baby Food: Steam extra asparagus and blend with stock. Omit the salt for the baby's portion and flake the salmon to be eaten as finger food. Serve with a side of mashed avocado.

Pork Meatball Soup

Serves: 4
Prep time: 15 minutes
Cook time: 30 minutes

Ingredients:

- 5 Tbsp. homemade ghee
- 1 onion, chopped
- 1 tsp. mineral salt
- 2 cloves garlic, chopped
- 5 cups homemade meat stock
- 1 lb. organic pasture-raised ground pork
- 2 zucchinis, sliced
- 2 cups kale, chopped
- Sauerkraut as tolerated

Directions:

1. In a bowl, combine the pork, garlic, onion and salt. Form into 16 meatballs and set aside.
2. In a large pot, melt the ghee over a medium heat. Add the vegetables and cover with a lid. Cook for 20-30 minutes or until the vegetables are soft.
3. In a separate pot, add the meat stock and the meatballs and bring to a boil. Reduce to a simmer, and cook for 30 minutes or until the meatballs are cooked through. Add the cooked vegetables to the soup.
4. Serve with a side of sauerkraut. Enjoy however much is tolerated.

Storage: Store any leftover soup in an airtight container in the fridge for up to 3 days.

Baby Food: Boil some zucchini and kale separately in salt-free, homemade meat stock and then purée. The meatballs can also be cut into strips and served as finger food if the salt is omitted.

Chicken and Green Bean Stew

Serves: 4
Prep time: 5 minutes
Cook time: 25-30 minutes

Ingredients:

- 4 Tbsp. homemade grass-fed ghee
- 1 onion, sliced
- 2 garlic cloves, chopped
- 1 lb. organic pasture-raised chicken thighs, cooked (you can use the chicken that was cooked while making the homemade meat stock)
- ½ tsp. mineral salt
- 2 cups homemade meat stock
- 1 lb. green beans, chopped
- ½ avocado, mashed

Directions:

1. Add the ghee to a stockpot over a medium heat and add the vegetables. Cover with a lid and cook for 20 minutes or until soft.
2. Add the meat stock to the pot along with the cooked chicken thighs. Cook for an additional 5-10 minutes or until the cooked chicken is warmed through.
3. Serve with mashed avocado.

Storage: Store any leftovers in an airtight container in the fridge for up to 3-4 days.

Baby Food: Omit the salt and serve warm without the chicken thighs or steam extra vegetables and blend with stock. Cut up a boneless and skinless chicken thigh cooked in homemade meat stock as finger food.

Ginger Chicken and Bok Choy Soup

Serves: 4
Prep time: 5 minutes
Cook time: 30 minutes

Ingredients:

- 4 Tbsp. homemade ghee
- 4 cups homemade meat stock
- 1 tsp. mineral salt
- 4-inch piece of ginger, sliced
- 1 lb. organic pasture-raised chicken thighs
- 1 large carrot, sliced
- 2 heads baby bok choy, chopped
- Sauerkraut as tolerated

Directions:

1. In a large pot over high heat, add the stock, salt and ginger. Bring to a boil, then reduce the heat to allow it to simmer.
2. Add the chicken to the pot and simmer for about 20 minutes or until the chicken is cooked through.
3. While the chicken is cooking, add the ghee to a stockpot over a medium heat and add the vegetables. Cover with a lid and cook for 20 minutes or until soft.
4. Transfer the chicken to a cutting board and shred or cut into strips then return to the pot.
5. Enjoy with a side of sauerkraut as tolerated. Some people start with a drop while others do ok with a teaspoon.

Storage: Store any leftovers in an airtight container in the fridge for up to 3 days.

Baby Food: Omit the salt and serve warm or steam extra vegetables and blend with some stock. Serve strips of the boneless, skinless chicken thigh as finger food.

STAGE 4

Tuscan Veggie Frittata

Serves: 4
Prep time: 10 minutes
Cook time: 32 minutes

Ingredients:

- 8 organic pasture-raised eggs
- ¼ cup homemade yogurt
- 1 tsp. dried oregano
- ½ cup fresh chopped parsley, chopped
- 2 Tbsp. homemade grass-fed ghee
- ½ small onion, sliced
- ½ tsp. mineral salt
- 1 cup kale, chopped
- 1 zucchini, sliced
- 2 cloves garlic, minced
- 1 avocado, sliced

Directions:

1. Preheat the oven to 325°F.
2. In a large bowl, whisk together the eggs, yogurt, oregano, salt and parsley. Set aside.
3. In a large ovenproof skillet (cast-iron is best), melt the ghee over a low heat. Add the onion and sauté until softened, for about 10 minutes.
4. Add the zucchini, kale and garlic and cook, stirring frequently, for about 1 minute.
5. Pour the egg mixture into the pan and let it cook over a medium heat for 2 minutes.
6. Transfer to the oven and bake for about 20 minutes, or until the eggs have set in the center.
7. Serve with a side of sliced avocado or a drizzle of high-quality cold pressed olive oil.

Storage: Store any leftovers in an airtight container in the fridge for up to 3 days.

Baby Food: Set some vegetables aside to cook separately and purée with some salt-free, homemade stock. Alternatively, especially if doing baby-led weaning, omit the salt and chop the frittata into thin strips as finger food.

Sunshine Smoothie

Serves: 4
Prep time: 10 minutes
Cook time: 0 minutes

Ingredients:

- 1 cup filtered water
- ½ cup homemade carrot juice
- ½ cup pumpkin, cooked
- ¼ cup homemade yogurt
- 1 egg yolk
- 1 Tbsp. almond butter

Directions:

1. Add all of the ingredients to a blender and blend until smooth.
2. Enjoy immediately or store it in the fridge.

Storage: Store any leftover smoothie in an airtight container in the fridge for up to 2 days. Simply stir the smoothie before drinking.

Baby Food: Omit the egg yolk and almond butter.

Almond Butter Pancakes

Serves: 4
Prep time: 10 minutes
Cook time: 10 minutes

Ingredients:

- 1 cup pumpkin or summer squash, cooked and puréed
- ⅓ cup organic almond butter
- ½ cup homemade almond flour
- 5 eggs, yolks and whites separated
- 1 Tbsp. raw honey
- ¼ tsp. mineral salt
- Grass-fed ghee, for cooking

Directions:

1. In a bowl, beat the egg whites until it starts to stiffen and form soft peaks.
2. In a separate bowl, whisk together the pumpkin, almond butter, almond flour, egg yolks, honey and salt. Fold in the egg whites gently. The batter should be light and fluffy.
3. In a large skillet, melt enough ghee to coat the pan over a low heat. Scoop the batter into the pan to form small pancakes.
4. Cook for about 2-3 minutes per side, being careful not to let it burn.
5. Enjoy warm, topped with more ghee and honey, if desired.

Storage: Store any leftovers in an airtight container in the fridge for up to 5 days.

Baby Food: This recipe can be enjoyed if the baby is able to have honey (over age 1) and almond butter.

Lunchbox/Picnic: Pack these pancakes in an airtight Ziploc bag or container for the perfect snack.

Chicken with Minty Cauli-Rice

Serves: 4
Prep time: 10 minutes
Cook time: 5 minutes

Ingredients:

- ½ cup homemade chicken meat stock
- 1 head cauliflower, cut into florets
- ½ cup fresh mint, chopped
- Sauerkraut juice as tolerated
- 2 Tbsp. homemade ghee
- ¼ tsp. mineral salt
- 2 cups organic pasture-raised chicken, cooked (in stock) and shredded
- 1 organic pasture-raised egg yolk

Directions:

1. Add the cauliflower to a food processor and pulse until it starts to resemble rice.
2. In a large skillet, heat the stock over a medium heat. Once it starts to simmer, add the cauliflower. Cover and let it cook for 5 minutes or until the cauliflower is cooked.
3. Remove from the heat and mix in the mint, sauerkraut juice, ghee and salt. Add as much sauerkraut juice as tolerated. Some people start with a drop while others do ok with a teaspoon.
4. Top with the shredded chicken and an egg yolk.

Storage: Store any leftovers in an airtight container in the fridge for up to 3 days.

Baby Food: Set aside extra cauliflower rice and purée with other steamed vegetables and stock or omit the salt and serve without the egg yolk if doing baby-led weaning.

Green Monster Chicken Salad

Serves: 2
Prep time: 10 minutes
Cook time: 0 minutes

Ingredients:

- ½ avocado
- 2 organic pasture-raised boneless and skinless chicken thighs, cooked in meat stock and shredded
- ¼ cup fresh herbs, chopped (or 2 Tbsp. dried herbs)
- 2 Tbsp. homemade yogurt (if tolerated)
- 1 tsp. cold pressed olive oil
- ¼ tsp. mineral salt
- ¼ tsp. black pepper, freshly ground

Directions:

1. In a small bowl, add the avocado and use a fork to mash the avocado.
2. Add the chicken, herbs, yogurt (if using), lemon or lime juice, olive oil, salt and pepper. Mix thoroughly to combine.
3. Enjoy on top of a slice of GAPS-approved almond flour bread.

Storage: Store any leftovers in an airtight container in the fridge for up to 3 days.

Baby Food: Mash the avocado and mix with chicken strips for finger food. Alternatively, simply omit the salt.

Squash Fries with Homemade Herb Aioli

Serves: 4
Prep time: 10 minutes
Cook time: 15-20 minutes

Ingredients:

For the fries:

- 1 medium summer squash, peeled and cut into wedges
- 2 Tbsp. coconut oil
- 1 tsp. mineral salt

For the aioli:

- 3 egg yolks
- ½-¾ cup cold pressed olive oil
- 1 cup fresh herbs, chopped
- ½ tsp. mineral salt

Directions:

1. Preheat the oven to 350°F. Line a baking sheet with parchment paper.
2. Add the squash to the baking sheet and toss with the coconut oil and salt.
3. Roast in the oven for 15-20 minutes, flipping halfway through, or until the squash is cooked.
4. To make the aioli, add the egg yolks and salt to a blender and blend until smooth. With the blender on, slowly drizzle in the oil to emulsify. Add the herbs and salt and pulse to combine.

Storage: Store any leftover fries in an airtight container in the fridge for up to 3 days. Store the aioli in an airtight container in the fridge for up to 2 days.

Baby Food: These fries are the perfect baby food if you omit the salt and aioli.

Lunchbox/Picnic: Pack these fries with aioli in an insulated lunchbox or cooler on ice.

Kraut Burgers with Avocado Sauce

Serves: 4
Prep time: 15 minutes
Cook time: 6-10 minutes

Ingredients:

- 1 lb. organic grass-fed ground beef
- 1 cup fresh chopped cilantro, chopped and divided
- 1 organic pasture-raised egg
- 1 clove garlic, chopped
- 1 tsp. mineral salt, divided
- 2 avocados, pitted and peeled
- 2 Tbsp. water
- Sauerkraut as tolerated
- Homemade ghee for cooking

Directions:

1. In a large bowl, mix together the ground beef, half a cup of cilantro, egg, garlic and half a teaspoon of salt. Form into 4 large patties, putting a slight indentation in the center of each patty to keep it from swelling up during cooking.
2. Cook the patties over a medium heat in a pan with the ghee and cook for 3-5 minutes on each side, or until well done.
3. In a blender, add the avocado, water, the remaining half cup of cilantro and the remaining half teaspoon of salt. Blend until smooth.
4. Serve the burgers topped with sauerkraut and avocado sauce. Use as much sauerkraut as tolerated. Some people start with a drop while others do ok with a teaspoon.

Storage: Store any leftover burgers or avocado sauce in an airtight container in the fridge for up to 2 days.

Baby Food: Cut a burger into strips and serve with some mashed avocado.

Wild Cod and Veggie Bake

Serves: 4
Prep time: 10 minutes
Cook time: 12-15 minutes

Ingredients:

- 1.5 lb. wild cod, chopped
- 2 zucchinis, chopped
- 1 cup green beans, chopped
- 1 tsp. mineral salt
- ¼ cup homemade ghee, melted
- 4 organic pasture-raised egg yolks

Directions:

1. Preheat the oven to 375°F.
2. Add the cod, zucchinis, green beans, ghee and salt to a casserole dish and toss to coat everything with the ghee.
3. Bake in the oven for 12-15 minutes or until the vegetables and fish are cooked through.
4. Serve topped with egg yolks.

Storage: Store any leftovers in an airtight container in the fridge for up to 3 days.

Baby Food: Cook extra vegetables on the stove in salt-free, homemade stock and purée until smooth.

STAGE 5

Chicken Tenders

Serves: 4
Prep time: 10 minutes
Cook time: 30 minutes

Ingredients:

- 1 lb. organic pasture-raised boneless and skinless chicken thighs, cut into tenders
- 2 organic, pasture-raised eggs
- 1 cup almond flour
- 1 tsp. mineral salt
- 1 tsp. dried oregano

Directions:

1. Preheat the oven to 375°F. Line a baking sheet with parchment paper
2. Add the eggs to a small shallow bowl and whisk.
3. In another small shallow bowl, mix together the almond flour, salt and oregano.
4. Coat the chicken tenders in the egg mixture and then the almond flour mixture. Place them on the baking sheet. Repeat with the remaining tenders.
5. Bake for 30 minutes, or until the chicken is completely cooked through, flipping halfway through.
6. Enjoy with a side of squash fries.

Storage: Store any leftovers in an airtight container in the fridge for up to 3 days or in the freezer for up to a month.

Baby Food: Cut the tenders into strips to make them baby-friendly.

Lunchbox/Picnic: Pack these in an insulated lunchbox or cooler on ice.

Basic Almond Flour Bread

Serves: 8
Prep time: 15 minutes
Cook time: 45-60 minutes

Ingredients:

- 2 ½ cups homemade almond flour
- 3 organic pasture-raised eggs
- 2 Tbsp. coconut oil, melted
- 2 Tbsp. homemade ghee, melted
- ½ tsp. mineral salt

Directions:

1. Preheat the oven to 350°F. Grease a loaf pan with ghee or coconut oil.
2. Add all of the ingredients to a bowl and mix to combine.
3. Pour the mixture into the loaf pan and spread into one even layer.
4. Bake for 45-60 minutes or until a knife inserted into the center comes out clean.
5. Allow the bread to cool before slicing. Serve with a drizzle of cold pressed olive oil, if desired.

Storage: Store the bread in an airtight container in the fridge for up to 5 days.

Baby Food: Cut the bread into bite-sized pieces as finger food (if not avoiding nuts).

Lunchbox/Picnic: Bring this bread on a picnic and use it as a sandwich base for vegetables and meats.

Carrot Mango Smoothie

Serves: 4
Prep time: 10 minutes
Cook time: 0 minutes

Ingredients:

- 1 cup fresh carrot juice
- 1 cup filtered water
- 1 cup mango
- 1 Tbsp. almond butter

Directions:

1. Add all of the ingredients to a high-speed blender and blend until smooth.

Storage: Store any leftover smoothie in an airtight container in the fridge up to 2 days. Stir before drinking.

Baby Food: Omit the almond butter for a baby-friendly smoothie.

Lunchbox/Picnic: Freeze the smoothie in individual cups and pack in a lunchbox or for a picnic.

Apples and Almond Butter Breakfast Bowl

Serves: 4
Prep time: 10 minutes
Cook time: 15 minutes

Ingredients:

- 1 Tbsp. homemade ghee
- 2 apples, peeled, cored and chopped
- ¼ cup organic almond butter
- 1 Tbsp. raw honey
- ¼ tsp. mineral salt

Directions:

1. In a large pot over a medium heat, melt the ghee. Add the apples and cook for 15 minutes, or until the apples turn mushy.
2. Transfer the apples to a high-speed blender. Add the honey and salt, and blend until smooth.
3. Serve the purée topped with almond butter.

Storage: Store any leftovers in an airtight container in the fridge for up to 3 days.

Baby Food: Serve plain puréed apples to your baby.

Salmon Lettuce Cups with Cilantro Avocado Sauce

Serves: 4
Prep time: 10 minutes
Cook time: 10-12 minutes

Ingredients:

- 1 lb. wild-caught salmon
- 2 avocados
- ¼ cup cilantro
- 2 Tbsp. homemade meat stock
- 1 tsp. ground cumin
- ½ tsp. mineral salt
- 1 large head butter lettuce
- Sauerkraut as tolerated

Directions:

1. Preheat the oven to 400°F. Line a baking sheet with parchment paper.
2. Add the salmon to the baking sheet and sprinkle with salt. Bake for 10-12 minutes, or until cooked through.
3. In the meantime, add the avocado, cilantro, stock, cumin and salt to a blender, and blend until smooth.
4. Break the salmon into pieces and place inside the butter lettuce leaves.
5. Serve topped with avocado sauce and sauerkraut as tolerated.

Storage: Store any leftover salmon or avocado sauce in an airtight container for up to 2 days.

Baby Food: Serve the roasted salmon, cut into bite-sized pieces, with a side of mashed avocado.

Cucumber Ribbons with Creamy Dill Dressing

Serves: 4
Prep time: 15 minutes
Cook time: 0 minutes

Ingredients:

- 2 Tbsp. cold pressed olive oil
- 1 Tbsp. homemade yogurt
- 1 Tbsp. lemon juice
- ½ tsp. mineral salt
- 2 large cucumbers, skin removed and peeled into ribbons
- ½ cup fresh dill

Directions:

1. Add the oil, yogurt, lemon and salt to a bowl, and whisk to combine.
2. Add the cucumber and dill to the bowl, and stir to combine.

Storage: Store any leftover salad in an airtight container for up to 3 days.

Baby Food: Cut the cucumber into small strips for your baby.

Lunchbox/Picnic: Store this salad in an airtight container in a cooler pack to pack for lunch or a picnic.

Baked Cabbage Rolls

Serves: 4
Prep time: 15 minutes
Cook time: 30 minutes

Ingredients:

- 1 head cabbage
- 1 lb. grass-fed ground beef
- 1 organic pasture-raised egg
- 2 cloves garlic, chopped
- 1 tsp. ground cumin
- 1 tsp. ground paprika
- 1 tsp. mineral salt
- 1 cup homemade meat stock
- Sauerkraut as tolerated

Directions:

1. Preheat the oven to 350°F. Lightly grease a casserole dish with oil.
2. In a large bowl, mix together the beef, egg, garlic, cumin, paprika and salt.
3. Remove the large leaves from the cabbage and lay out on a cutting board. Place a quarter of a cup of the ground beef mixture into the center of the cabbage leaf. Roll the leaf as if rolling a burrito and place into the baking dish.
4. Repeat with each cabbage leaf until ground beef is used up. Pour the homemade stock over the rolls and bake for 30 minutes, or until the beef is cooked through.
5. Serve with sauerkraut as tolerated.

Storage: Store any leftover cabbage rolls in an airtight container in the fridge for up to 3 days.

Baby Food: Make small patties with the ground beef mixture (minus the salt) and cook in a pan with some ghee. Cut into strips to serve to your baby.

Lunchbox/Picnic: Pack these rolls in an airtight container on ice in an insulated lunchbox or cooler.

Baked Moroccan Lamb Meatballs and Cauliflower

Serves: 4
Prep time: 15 minutes
Cook time: 30 minutes

Ingredients:

- 1 lb. grass-fed ground lamb
- 1 organic pasture-raised egg
- 1 tsp. ground cumin
- 1 tsp. mineral salt, divided
- ½ tsp. ground cinnamon
- ½ tsp. ground paprika
- 3 cups cauliflower florets
- 1 Tbsp. coconut oil, melted

Directions:

1. Preheat the oven to 350°F. Line a baking sheet with parchment paper.
2. In a large bowl, mix together the lamb, egg, cumin, half a teaspoon of salt, cinnamon and paprika. Roll into meatballs and place on half of the baking sheet.
3. Add the cauliflower to the other half of the sheet and drizzle with coconut oil and the remaining half teaspoon of salt.
4. Bake for 30 minutes, or until the meatballs and cauliflower are cooked through.

Storage: Store any leftover meatballs in an airtight container in the fridge for up to 3 days.

Baby Food: Make separate lamb patties without the salt and roast on a separate baking sheet with some cauliflower. Cut into finger food pieces for your baby.

Roasted Chicken and Carrots with Chimichurri Sauce

Serves: 4
Prep time: 10 minutes
Cook time: 30 minutes

Ingredients:

- 1 lb. organic chicken thighs, boneless and skinless
- 8 large carrots
- 2 Tbsp. coconut oil, melted
- 1 ½ tsp. mineral salt, divided
- ½ cup mint, chopped
- ½ cup cilantro, chopped
- ¼ cup olive oil
- 1 Tbsp. lemon juice

Directions:

1. Preheat the oven to 375°F. Line a baking sheet with parchment paper.
2. Place the chicken thighs and whole carrots on the baking sheet and drizzle with the melted coconut oil and sprinkle with 1 teaspoon of salt.
3. Bake for 30 minutes, or until chicken and carrots are cooked through.
4. To make the chimichurri, add the mint, cilantro, olive oil, lemon juice and the remaining half teaspoon of salt to a bowl and whisk to combine.
5. Serve the chicken and carrots topped with chimichurri.

Storage: Store any leftover chicken in an airtight container in the fridge for up to 2 days.

Baby Food: Omit the salt, and before you add the chimichurri, cut up the chicken and carrots into bite-sized pieces for your baby.

Greek Lettuce Tacos with Tzatziki Sauce

Serves: 4
Prep time: 15 minutes
Cook time: 10 minutes

Ingredients:

- 1 Tbsp. homemade ghee
- 1 onion, chopped
- 2 tsp. mineral salt, divided
- 1 lb. grass-fed ground beef
- 1 tsp. ground cumin
- ¼ cup parsley, chopped
- 1 cup homemade yogurt
- 1 cucumber, peeled and finely chopped
- ½ cup mint, chopped
- 1 Tbsp. lemon juice
- 1 clove garlic, minced
- 1 head butter lettuce
- 1 tomato, chopped

Directions:

1. In a large skillet, melt the ghee over a medium heat. Add the onion and 1 teaspoon of salt and cook until softened, for about 5 minutes. Add the beef, cumin and parsley and cook, breaking the meat up, for about 10 minutes or until cooked through.
2. To make the sauce, add the yogurt, cucumber, mint, lemon juice, garlic and the remaining 1 teaspoon of salt to a bowl and mix to combine.
3. Scoop the beef mixture into a lettuce leaf and top with the tzatziki and chopped tomato.

Storage: Store any leftover beef in an airtight container in the fridge for up to 3 days. Store any leftover tzatziki in an airtight container for up to 5 days.

Baby Food: Make separate beef patties minus the salt and cook separately. Cut into finger food pieces for your baby.

Lunchbox/Picnic: Pack the lettuce, beef and tzatziki separately in airtight containers and pack on ice in a lunch box or cooler for a picnic.

Lamb Ratatouille

Serves: 4
Prep time: 10 minutes
Cook time: 10 minutes

Ingredients:

- 3 cups homemade meat stock
- 1 medium onion, sliced
- 2 cloves garlic
- ½ tsp. mineral salt
- 2 tomatoes, chopped (omit if you are sensitive to nightshade vegetables)
- 1 eggplant, cubed
- 2 large carrots, sliced
- 1 large zucchini, sliced
- 2 rosemary sprigs
- 1 lb. grass-fed lamb, cooked (in homemade meat stock) and cubed
- Homemade sauerkraut juice as tolerated

Directions:

1. In a large pot, add the stock, onion, garlic and salt. Cook for 5 minutes or until the onion softens. Add the tomatoes, eggplant, carrots, zucchini and rosemary.
2. Add the cooked lamb meat and stir. If there is not enough liquid, add some more stock. Simmer for another 5 minutes.
3. Remove the rosemary sprigs and serve with sauerkraut juice as tolerated.

Storage: Store any leftovers in an airtight container in the fridge for up to 3-4 days.

Baby Food: Add the salt to the recipe once you have set aside a portion for the baby. Alternatively, set aside extra vegetables and boil in some stock, then purée until smooth or serve the cooked vegetables as finger food if doing baby-led weaning.

Lamb Garlic Meatballs with Cauliflower Mash

Serves: 4
Prep time: 15 minutes
Cook time: 25-30 minutes

Ingredients:

- 1 lb. ground lamb
- 2 cloves garlic, chopped
- ½ tsp. mineral salt
- 3 cups homemade meat stock
- 2 tomatoes, chopped
- 2 cups cauliflower florets
- Homemade sauerkraut juice as tolerated.

Directions:

1. In a bowl, combine the lamb, garlic and salt. Form into 16 meatballs and set aside.
2. In a large pot, add the stock and tomatoes. Bring to a boil, then reduce the heat to low. Add the lamb meatballs and simmer, covered, for 15-20 minutes or until the meatballs are cooked through.
3. Once the meatballs are cooked, remove them from the pot. Simmer the stock and tomatoes uncovered for 10 minutes to thicken.
4. In the meantime, steam the cauliflower in a separate pot until very soft. Remove from the pot and transfer to a bowl. Mash with a fork or masher.
5. Serve the meatballs and cauliflower mash topped with the tomato and stock liquid.
6. Enjoy with sauerkraut juice, only adding however much you can tolerate.

Storage: Store any leftover lamb meatballs in an airtight container in the fridge for up to 3-4 days or in the freezer for up to a month. Leftover cauliflower mash can be stored for up to 5 days in the fridge.

Baby Food: Set aside the mashed cauliflower and mix it with a little bit of salt-free, homemade stock.

Beef & Veggie Stew

Serves: 4
Prep time: 10 minutes
Cook time: 30 minutes

Ingredients:

- 4 cups homemade meat stock
- 2 cloves garlic
- ½ tsp. mineral salt
- 1 onion, sliced
- 2 large carrots, chopped
- 3 tomatoes, chopped (omit if sensitive to nightshade vegetables)
- 2 cups broccoli florets
- 1 lb. organic grass-fed ground beef, cut into bite-sized chunks
- Homemade sauerkraut juice as tolerated.

Directions:

1. In a large pot, add the stock, garlic, salt and onion. Bring to a boil, then reduce heat to low.
2. Add the carrots, tomatoes, broccoli and beef chunks to the pot and simmer for 25 minutes or until the vegetables and beef are cooked through.
3. Serve with sauerkraut juice. Enjoy however much is tolerated.

Storage: Store any leftover stew in an airtight container in the fridge for up to 3-4 days or in the freezer for up to a month.

Baby Food: Steam extra broccoli and carrots separately and purée with homemade meat stock.

Creamy Eggplant Soup

Serves: 4
Prep time: 5 minutes
Cook time: 30 minutes

Ingredients:

- 4 cups homemade meat stock
- 2 cups water
- 2 cloves garlic
- ½ tsp. Celtic sea salt
- 1 Tbsp. homemade ghee
- 2 cups eggplant, cubed
- 1 cup cauliflower florets
- ¼ cup homemade yogurt (if not tolerated, go back to Stage 1)

Directions:

1. In a large pot, add the stock, water, garlic, salt, ghee, eggplant and cauliflower. If everything is not completely covered, add more stock or water.
2. Bring to a boil, then reduce the heat to low and simmer for 30 minutes or until the vegetables are cooked through.
3. Purée the soup until smooth. Top with a dollop of homemade yogurt.

Storage: Store any leftover soup in an airtight container in the fridge for up to 3-4 days or in the freezer for up to a month.

Baby Food: Boil in salt-free, homemade stock and then purée extra eggplant and cauliflower separately.

Lunchbox/Picnic: This soup is great cold. Pack in an insulated lunch box or cooler with an ice pack.

Chicken Enchilada Stew

Serves: 4
Prep time: 10 minutes
Cook time: 30 minutes

Ingredients:

- 2 Tbsp. homemade ghee
- 1 onion, sliced
- 2 cups spinach, chopped
- 4 tomatoes, chopped (omit if sensitive to nightshade vegetables)
- 1 red bell pepper, chopped (omit if sensitive to nightshade vegetables)
- 2 cup homemade meat stock
- 2 garlic cloves, chopped
- 1 sprig of fresh oregano
- ½ tsp. mineral salt
- 1 lb. organic pasture-raised chicken, cooked (in stock) and shredded
- ½ avocado, mashed

Directions:

1. In a large stockpot, melt the ghee over a low heat.
2. Add the onion, spinach, tomatoes, red pepper, stock, garlic, oregano and salt. Simmer until the sauce thickens, for about 20 minutes. Add the chicken and cook until heated through. Remove the oregano sprig from the pot.
3. Serve with mashed avocado.

Storage: Store any leftovers in an airtight container in the fridge for up to 3-4 days.

Baby Food: Steam extra vegetables and blend with salt-free, homemade stock. Cut up a boneless, skinless chicken thigh cooked in meat stock as finger food and serve with mashed avocado.

Chicken and Cabbage Stew

Serves: 4
Prep time: 5 minutes
Cook time: 30 minutes

Ingredients:

- 2 Tbsp. homemade ghee
- 1 onion, sliced
- 2 carrots, chopped
- 1 tsp. mineral salt, divided in half
- 4 cups homemade meat stock
- ½ head cabbage, chopped
- 3 cloves garlic
- 4 organic pasture-raised chicken thighs, cooked (you can use the meat from the chicken you used to make the homemade meat stock)
- Sauerkraut as tolerated

Directions:

1. In a large stockpot, melt the ghee over a low heat. Add all of the ingredients minus the cooked chicken and bring to a simmer.
2. Simmer for 20 minutes or until the vegetables are tender.
3. Stir in the cooked chicken and cook for an additional 10 minutes or until warmed through.
4. Serve with a side of sauerkraut - however much is tolerated.

Storage: Store any leftovers in an airtight container in the fridge for up to 3-4 days.

Baby Food: Steam extra vegetables and blend with the homemade meat stock. Cut up a boneless, skinless chicken thigh (cooked in meat stock) and serve as finger food.

Celeriac Soup

Serves: 4
Prep time: 5 minutes
Cook time: 30 minutes

Ingredients:

- 4 cups homemade meat stock
- 2 cups filtered water
- 2 cloves garlic
- ½ tsp. mineral salt
- 1 Tbsp. homemade ghee
- 1 cup celeriac, peeled and cubed
- 1 cup celery, chopped
- 1 cup cauliflower florets

Directions:

1. In a large pot, add the stock, water, garlic, salt, ghee, celeriac, celery and cauliflower. If everything is not completely covered, add more stock or water.
2. Bring to a boil, then reduce the heat to low and simmer for 30 minutes or until the vegetables are cooked and tender.
3. Purée the soup until smooth.

Storage: Store any leftover soup in an airtight container in the fridge for up to 3-4 days or in the freezer for up to a month.

Baby Food: Omit the salt and serve warm or cold.

Lunchbox/Picnic: This soup is great cold. Pack in an insulated lunch box or cooler with an ice pack.

Greek Stuffed Zucchini Boats

Serves: 4
Prep time: 10 minutes
Cook time: 30-45 minutes

Ingredients:

- 3-4 large zucchini, cut lengthwise
- 1 lb. organic pasture-raised ground turkey
- 1 tomato, chopped
- ½ cup parsley, chopped
- 2 organic pasture-raised eggs
- 2 cloves garlic, chopped
- 1 tsp. dried oregano
- ½ tsp. mineral salt
- 1 Tbsp. cold pressed olive oil

Directions:

1. Preheat the oven to 350°F. Line a baking sheet with parchment paper.
2. Use a spoon to scoop the flesh out of the center of the zucchini halves to create 'boats'. Use a vegetable peeler or knife to remove a thin strip from the back of the zucchini so it stays in place.
3. In a bowl, mix together the turkey, tomato, parsley, eggs, garlic, oregano and salt.
4. Divide the mixture into each zucchini boat.
5. Bake for 30-45 minutes, or until the meat is cooked through.
6. Serve drizzled with olive oil.

Storage: Store any leftovers in an airtight container in the fridge for up to 2 days.

Baby Food: Roast a zucchini separately and cut up into finger food for your baby or simply omit the salt and then chop up the zucchini boat into strips.

Lunchbox/Picnic: Pack these zucchini boats in an airtight container and place inside of your insulated lunchbox or cooler with an icepack.

STAGE 6

Apple and Almond Butter Smoothie

Serves: 1
Prep time: 5 minutes
Cook time: 0 minutes

Ingredients:

- 1 cup filtered water
- 1 cup homemade coconut milk
- ½ apple, peeled
- 2 Tbsp. almond butter
- ¼ cup homemade yogurt

Directions:

1. Add all of the ingredients into a high-speed blender and blend until smooth. If the smoothie is too thick, add more coconut milk or water.
2. Pour into a glass and enjoy straight away.

Storage: Store any leftover smoothie in the fridge for up to 2 days. Stir before drinking.

Baby Food: Omit the almond butter and yogurt to make a dairy- and nut-free version

Lunchbox/Picnic: Freeze the smoothie in an airtight container and pack in an insulated lunchbox or cooler.

Roasted Veggie Frittata Muffins

Serves: 4
Prep time: 10 minutes
Cook time: 35-40 minutes

Ingredients:

- 9 organic pasture-raised eggs
- 1 tsp. dried oregano
- ¼ tsp. mineral salt
- ½ cup kale, chopped
- ½ cup fresh parsley, chopped
- 1 cup pumpkin, cubed and roasted
- Sliced avocado (for serving)

Directions:

1. Preheat the oven to 350°F and line a standard muffin tin with muffin cups.
2. In a large bowl, whisk together the eggs, oregano and salt. Mix in the parsley, kale and pumpkin.
3. Divide the egg mixture into the muffin tin. Bake for 35-40 minutes, or until the eggs have set.
4. Enjoy with a side of avocado.

Storage: Store any leftover frittata muffins in an airtight container for up to 5 days.

Baby Food: Cut the frittata muffin into small strips for your baby.

Lunchbox/Picnic: Pack these in an airtight container in on ice in an insulated lunchbox or cooler.

Banana Bread Pancakes

Serves: 4
Prep time: 10 minutes
Cook time: 4-6 minutes

Ingredients:

- 1 cup mashed banana
- ½ cup almond butter
- 4 organic pasture-raised eggs
- ½ tsp. ground cinnamon
- ¼ tsp. mineral salt
- 2 Tbsp. homemade ghee

Directions:

1. In a bowl, mix together the banana, almond butter, eggs, cinnamon and salt.
2. In a large skillet, melt the ghee over a medium to low heat. Scoop the batter into the pan to form small pancakes.
3. Cook for about 2-3 minutes per side, being careful not to let it burn.
4. Enjoy warm.

Storage: Store any leftovers in an airtight container in the fridge for up to 5 days.

Baby Food: Cut the pancakes into thin strips as finger food, and omit the almond butter for a nut-free version.

Creamy Tomato Soup

Serves: 4
Prep time: 5 minutes
Cook time: 30 minutes

Ingredients:

- 4 cups homemade meat stock
- 3 cups homemade tomato purée
- 1 cup homemade coconut milk
- ½ tsp. mineral salt
- 1 Tbsp. homemade ghee
- 1 cup fresh basil, chopped
- Homemade yogurt (for serving)

Directions:

1. In a large pot, add the stock, tomato purée, coconut milk, salt, ghee and basil.
2. Bring to a boil, then reduce the heat to low and simmer for 30 minutes, or until the soup has thickened
3. Serve with a dollop of homemade yogurt on top.

Storage: Store any leftovers in an airtight container in the fridge for up to 5 days or in the freezer for up to a month.

Baby Food: This soup is great for babies. Omit the yogurt and ghee if dairy is not tolerated.

Picnic: This soup is also great cold to bring on a picnic or pack in a lunchbox.

Chicken Apple Salad

Serves: 4
Prep time: 10 minutes
Cook time: 0 minutes

Ingredients:

- 3 cups organic pasture-raised chicken breast, cooked and shredded
- 1 green apple, peeled, cored and roughly chopped
- 2 Tbsp. cold-pressed olive oil
- 1 Tbsp. homemade yogurt
- 1 tsp. lemon juice
- ½ tsp. mineral salt
- 2 cups lettuce, chopped, or leftover roasted vegetables

Directions:

1. In a medium bowl, add the chicken, apple, olive oil, yogurt, lemon juice and salt. Mix until thoroughly combined.
2. Serve on top of a bed of lettuce or leftover roasted vegetables.

Storage: Store any leftovers in an airtight container in the fridge for up to 3 days.

Baby Food: Set aside shredded chicken for your baby if avoiding dairy. Otherwise, omit the salt and walnuts.

Lunchbox/Picnic: Pack this salad in an airtight container on ice in an insulated lunchbox or cooler.

Carrot Noodles with Chicken and Ginger Almond Sauce

Serves: 4
Prep time: 15 minutes
Cook time: 3 minutes

Ingredients:

- 1 Tbsp. homemade ghee
- 5 carrots, peeled into 'ribbons'
- 1 tsp. mineral salt, divided
- 1 cup napa cabbage, thinly sliced
- 1 cup almond butter
- ¼ cup filtered water
- 1 Tbsp. lime juice
- 1 clove garlic, chopped
- 2-inch piece ginger, chopped
- 1 lb. organic boneless and skinless chicken thighs, cooked and shredded

Directions:

1. In a large skillet, melt the ghee over a medium heat. Add the carrot ribbons and 1 teaspoon of the salt. Sauté for 1 minute to soften then mix in the cabbage and set aside.
2. In a pot over a low heat, whisk together the almond butter, water, lime juice, garlic, ginger and the remaining 1 teaspoon of salt. If it is too thick, add more water until it is thin enough. Bring to a simmer for 2 minutes, then remove from heat.
3. Serve the carrot noodles and cabbage topped with shredded chicken and almond butter sauce

Storage: Store any leftover noodles and peanut sauce in separate airtight containers in the fridge for up to 3 days.

Baby Food: Steam some carrots separately and serve with shredded chicken.

Beef and Collard Green Stew

Serves: 4
Prep time: 15 minutes
Cook time: 10-15 minutes

Ingredients:

- 1 Tbsp. lard or homemade ghee
- 1 lb. grass-fed ground beef
- 1 tsp. mineral salt
- 1 cup homemade tomato purée
- 2 cloves garlic, chopped
- 4 cups collard greens, stems removed and chopped

Directions:

1. In a large skillet over a medium heat, melt the lard or ghee. Add the beef and salt and cook for 1 minute, mixing to break the meat up.
2. Add the tomato purée, garlic and collard greens and simmer for 10-15 minutes, or until cooked through.

Storage: Store any leftover stew in an airtight container in the fridge for up to 3 days.

Baby Food: Form extra beef into small patties and simmer in the stew. Cut up the patty as finger food.

Chicken Curry Soup

Serves: 4
Prep time: 10 minutes
Cook time: 35-37 minutes

Ingredients:

- 2 Tbsp. coconut oil
- 1 onion, chopped
- 2 cups broccoli florets
- 1 red bell pepper, chopped
- 2-inch piece of ginger, chopped
- 1 tsp. mineral salt
- 1 tsp. ground turmeric
- 1 tsp. ground cumin
- ¼ tsp. ground cinnamon
- 3 cups homemade coconut milk
- 1 cup homemade meat stock
- 4 organic chicken thighs, boneless and skinless
- Cilantro, for garnish

Directions:

1. In a large pot, melt the coconut oil over a medium heat. Add the onion, broccoli and bell pepper. Cook until softened, for about 5-7 minutes. Add the ginger, salt, turmeric, cumin and cinnamon and cook for 30 seconds, stirring frequently.
2. Add the coconut milk, stock and chicken. Bring to a boil, then reduce the heat to low and simmer, covered, for 30 minutes or until the chicken is cooked through.
3. Serve garnished with fresh, chopped cilantro.

Storage: Store any leftover soup in an airtight container in the fridge for up to 2 days.

Baby Food: Bake an extra chicken thigh and some vegetables in the oven and cut them up for your baby.

Purple Cabbage and Carrot Slaw

Serves: 4
Prep time: 10 minutes + chilling time
Cook time: 0 minutes

Ingredients:

- ½ large purple cabbage, thinly sliced
- 1 carrot, grated
- ½ cup cilantro, chopped
- 3 Tbsp. homemade yogurt
- 1 Tbsp. lime juice
- ½ tsp. mineral salt

Directions:

1. Add the cabbage, carrot, cilantro, yogurt, lime and salt to a bowl and mix to combine.
2. Allow the slaw to sit in the fridge for at least 1 hour to soften.

Storage: Store any leftover slaw in an airtight container for up to 5 days.

Baby Food: If the slaw is not suitable, set aside some vegetables to steam separately and purée with homemade stock.

FULL GAPS

BREAKFAST

Carrot Cake Breakfast Bites

Makes: 20 small cookies
Prep time: 10 minutes
Cook time: 10-12 minutes

Ingredients:

- 2 ½ cups homemade almond flour
- 1 cup carrots, grated
- ½ cup pecans, chopped
- ½ cup raisins
- 4 organic pasture-raised eggs
- 2 Tbsp. coconut oil, melted
- 1 Tbsp. raw honey
- 1 tsp. ground cinnamon
- ¼ tsp. mineral salt

Directions:

1. Preheat the oven to 350°F and line a baking sheet with parchment paper.
2. In a large bowl, mix together all of the ingredients until combined.
3. Scoop tablespoon-sized rounds onto the baking sheet. Bake for 10-12 minutes, or until the bottoms of the cookies are golden brown.
4. Allow to cool and enjoy as an easy breakfast.

Storage: Store any leftover cookies in an airtight container for up to 1 week, if they don't get eaten before then!

Baby Food: To make this recipe suitable for babies under 1, omit the honey. You could add an extra teaspoon of cinnamon to make it sweeter.

Lunchbox/Picnic: Pack these bites in a container for an easy snack or treat.

Egg Salad Stuffed Tomato

Serves: 4
Prep time: 10 minutes
Cook time: 0 minutes

Ingredients:

- 4 tomatoes
- 6 organic pasture-raised eggs, hard-boiled
- ½ cup walnuts, chopped
- ¼ cup fresh parsley, chopped
- 1 Tbsp. lemon juice
- 1 Tbsp. cold-pressed olive oil
- ¼ tsp. mineral salt

Directions:

1. Remove the stem and cut a hole in the top of the tomato, and use a spoon to scoop out the flesh.
2. In a medium bowl, add the eggs and mash with a fork. Mix in the walnuts, parsley, lemon juice, olive oil and salt.
3. Scoop the salad into each tomato and enjoy!

Storage: Store any leftovers in an airtight container in the fridge for up to 3 days.

Baby Food: Cut up some of the hard-boiled eggs for your baby or simply omit the salt and walnuts from the recipe.

Lunchbox/Picnic: Pack these in an airtight container on ice in an insulated lunchbox or cooler.

Herby Asparagus Parmesan Frittata

Serves: 4
Prep time: 5 minutes
Cook time: 30 minutes

Ingredients:

- 9 eggs
- ¼ cup homemade yogurt
- 1 tsp. dried oregano
- ½ cup parsley, chopped
- 2 Tbsp. coconut oil
- ½ small onion, sliced
- ½ tsp. mineral salt
- 1 bunch asparagus
- 2 cloves garlic, minced
- ½ cup Parmesan cheese

Directions:

1. Preheat the oven to 325°F.
2. In a large bowl, whisk together the eggs, yogurt, oregano and parsley. Set aside.
3. In a large ovenproof skillet (cast-iron is best), heat the coconut oil over a medium heat. Add the onion and sauté until softened, for about 5 minutes.
4. Add the asparagus and garlic and, stirring frequently, cook for about 1 minute.
5. Pour the egg mixture into the pan and cook over a medium heat for 5 minutes, or until the edges begin to set. Sprinkle the Parmesan cheese on top.
6. Transfer to the oven and bake for about 15 minutes, or until the eggs have set in the center and the top begins to turn golden. Cut into 8 slices and eat right away or let it cool completely and store in the fridge.

Storage: Store any leftovers in an airtight container in the fridge for up to 5 days or in the freezer for up to a month. For a quick breakfast, pop it out of the fridge or freezer and microwave it until warmed through.

Baby Food: Set some asparagus aside, steam it separately and purée it with some salt-free, homemade stock. Alternatively, especially if doing baby-led weaning, omit the salt and chop the frittata into thin strips as finger food.

Coconut Pumpkin Pancakes

Serves: 4
Prep time: 5 minutes
Cook time: 4-6 minutes

Ingredients:

- 5 organic pasture-raised eggs
- ½ cup coconut flour
- ⅓ cup coconut milk
- 2 Tbsp. homemade pumpkin purée
- 1 Tbsp. raw honey
- ½ tsp. mineral salt
- Coconut oil for cooking
- Homemade ghee (for serving)
- 1-2 tsp. cinnamon (for serving)

Directions:

1. Add all of the ingredients to a blender and blend until smooth.
2. In a large skillet over a medium heat, add enough coconut oil to coat the pan. Pour small pancakes into the pan and cook for 2-3 minutes per side.
3. Serve topped with a slab of butter and a sprinkle of cinnamon.

Storage: Store any leftover pancakes in an airtight container in the fridge for up to 3 days or in the freezer for up to a month. Simply pop the refrigerated or frozen pancake into your toaster and enjoy!

Baby Food: Make a little extra pumpkin purée and stir in a little coconut milk to use it as baby food. Alternatively, especially if doing baby-led weaning, omit the honey and salt from the recipe, cut the pancakes into thin strips and serve as finger food.

Papaya Pineapple Smoothie

Serves: 2
Prep time: 5 minutes
Cook time: 0 minutes

Ingredients:

- 1 cup papaya chunks
- 1 cup pineapple
- 2 cups baby spinach
- 1 cup homemade coconut milk
- ½ cup homemade yogurt
- 1 banana
- 1 Tbsp. almond butter

Directions:

1. Add all of the ingredients to a high-speed blender and blend until smooth.
2. Pour into a glass and enjoy straight away or store it in the fridge.

Storage: Make this smoothie the night before and store it in a bottle or jar with a lid in your fridge. Give it a good shake to remix and then sip on it in the morning.

Baby Food: This smoothie is great for babies. Omit the yogurt and almond butter if dairy and nuts are being avoided.

Berries and Cream Smoothie

Serves: 1
Prep time: 3 minutes
Cook time: 0 minutes

Ingredients:

- 1 cup raspberries
- 1 cup homemade coconut milk
- 1 cup baby spinach
- ½ cup homemade yogurt
- 1 banana
- 1 Tbsp. almond butter

Directions:

1. Add all of the ingredients to a high-speed blender and blend until smooth.
2. Pour it into a glass and enjoy straight away or store it in the fridge.

Storage: Make this smoothie the night before and store it in a bottle or jar with a lid in your fridge. Give it a good shake to remix and then sip on it in the morning.

Baby Food: This smoothie is great for babies. Omit the yogurt and almond butter if dairy and nuts are being avoided.

Honey Coconut Granola

Serves: 8
Prep time: 5 minutes
Cook time: 15 minutes

Ingredients:

- 1 cup raw almonds
- 1 cup raw cashews
- 1 cup raw walnuts
- 2 cups coconut flakes
- ¼ cup coconut oil, melted
- ¼ cup raw honey
- 1 tsp. vanilla extract
- ¼ tsp. mineral salt
- Homemade yogurt (for serving)
- Banana, sliced (for serving)

Directions:

1. Preheat the oven to 300°F. Line a baking sheet with parchment paper.
2. Add the nuts and coconut flakes to a large bowl.
3. In a small pot over a low heat, whisk together the coconut oil, honey, vanilla, and salt. Whisk together until the coconut oil is melted and mixed with the honey.
4. Pour the mixture over the nuts and toss to combine.
5. Bake for 15 minutes, stirring halfway through.
6. Allow to cool completely before storing or eating.
7. Enjoy on top of homemade yogurt and top with banana slices.

Storage: Store granola in an airtight container in a cool, dark place for up to 2 weeks.

Baby Food: This recipe is not adaptable if avoiding nuts. Finely chop the nuts if you have introduced nuts. Whole nuts should be avoided until at least 5 years old as they are a choking hazard.

Lunchbox/Picnic: This granola is a perfect packable snack for lunch or a picnic.

Banana Chocolate Shake

Serves: 1
Prep time: 3 minutes
Cook time: 0 minutes

Ingredients:

- 1 ripe banana, frozen
- 1 cup zucchini, steamed and cooled
- 2 Tbsp. raw unsweetened cocoa powder
- 1 Tbsp. almond butter
- ½ cup homemade almond milk

Directions:

1. Add all of the ingredients to a high-speed blender and blend until smooth.
2. Pour into a glass and enjoy straight away or store it in the fridge.

Storage: Make this smoothie the night before and store it in a bottle or jar with a lid in your fridge. Give it a good shake to remix and then sip on it in the morning.

Baby Food: Blend the banana and zucchini with your milk of choice for a baby-friendly version.

Pecan Pie Porridge

Serves: 2
Prep time: 5 minutes
Cook time: 10 minutes

Ingredients:

- 1 cup pecans, soaked overnight
- ¼ cup nut butter (almond or pecan)
- 1 ripe banana
- 2 organic pasture-raised eggs
- ½ cup homemade almond milk
- 2 tsp. raw honey (optional)
- ½ tsp. ground cinnamon
- ¼ tsp. ground ginger
- ¼ tsp. ground cloves
- 1 pinch mineral salt

Directions:

1. Add all of the ingredients to a high-speed blender and blend until smooth.
2. Transfer to a pot over a medium heat and simmer for 10 minutes, or until the porridge thickens.
3. Serve topped with more pecans and cinnamon.

Storage: Store any leftover porridge in an airtight container in the fridge for up to 1 week.

Baby Food: This recipe is not adaptable if avoiding nuts. Otherwise, omit the honey if the baby is under 1 and omit the salt.

Turkey Egg Scramble

Serves: 2
Prep time: 5 minutes
Cook time: 15-20 minutes

Ingredients:

- 1 Tbsp. coconut oil
- 1 onion, chopped
- ½ tsp. mineral salt
- ½ tsp. fennel seeds
- ½ tsp. dried oregano
- ½ lb. of ground turkey
- 3 cups baby spinach
- 4 organic pasture-raised eggs, whisked
- ¼ cup Parmesan cheese (optional)

Directions:

1. In a large skillet, heat the coconut oil over a medium heat. Add the onion, salt, fennel and oregano and cook for 5 minutes or until softened.
2. Add the ground turkey and cook for 7-10 minutes or until cooked through.
3. Add the spinach and eggs and cook, moving the eggs around, for 2-3 minutes or until eggs are cooked.
4. Serve topped with Parmesan cheese, if desired.

Storage: Store any leftover scramble in an airtight container in the fridge for up to 2 days.

Baby Food: Scramble eggs and cook turkey separately for your baby without the salt.

Kale and Swiss Cheese Breakfast Casserole

Serves: 4-6
Prep time: 10 minutes
Cook time: 30 minutes

Ingredients:

- 8 large organic pasture-raised eggs
- 1 tsp. mineral salt
- ½ cup homemade yogurt
- 5 cups kale, chopped
- 1 cup cherry tomatoes
- 2 cloves garlic, chopped
- 1 cup Swiss cheese, grated
- Homemade ghee or coconut oil for cooking

Directions:

1. Preheat the oven to 350°F. Grease a 9x13 baking dish with ghee or coconut oil.
2. In a bowl, whisk together the eggs, salt and yogurt. Set aside.
3. Add the kale, tomatoes and garlic to the baking dish and spread into an even layer.
4. Pour the egg mixture over top and shake so that the mixture settles. Top with Swiss cheese and bake for 30 minutes, or until eggs are set in the center.
5. Cut into squares and serve.

Storage: Store any leftover casserole in an airtight container in the fridge for up to 3 days.

Baby Food: Omit the salt, garlic, yogurt and cheese if avoiding dairy.

Lunchbox/Picnic: Pack some of the casserole squares in an airtight container on ice in an insulated lunchbox or cooler.

Squash Egg Basket

Serves: 2
Prep time: 10 minutes
Cook time: 30-35 minutes

Ingredients:

- 1 acorn or delicata squash, cut in half and seeds removed
- ½ tsp. mineral salt
- 2 organic pasture-raised eggs
- ½ avocado, sliced

Directions:

1. Preheat the oven to 350°F. Line a baking sheet with parchment paper.
2. Brush the cut-side of the squash with oil and sprinkle with sea salt. Place on the baking sheet.
3. Bake for 15 minutes. Remove from the oven and crack an egg into each hole.
4. Return to the oven and bake for an additional 15-20 minutes, or until the egg and squash are cooked through.
5. Serve with sliced avocado.

Storage: These do not store well once the egg is added, but it is helpful to have cooked squash in the fridge so that the recipe is quicker to make.

Baby Food: Cooked squash and egg are great for baby food, either mashed or cut into baby-friendly strips.

LUNCH

Chicken & Veg Nuggets

Serves: 4
Prep time: 15 minutes
Cook time: 20 minutes

Ingredients:

For the chicken:

- 1 lb. organic ground chicken
- 1 cup broccoli florets
- 2 carrots, chopped
- 1 organic pasture-raised egg
- 2 cloves garlic, minced
- ¼ cup almond flour
- ½ tsp. dried oregano
- ½ tsp. mineral salt

For the coating:

- 1 organic pasture-raised egg, whisked
- 1 cup almond flour
- 1 tsp. dried oregano
- ½ tsp. mineral salt

Directions:

1. Preheat the oven to 400°F. Line a baking sheet with lightly-greased parchment paper.
2. Add the carrots and broccoli to a food processor and pulse until everything is very finely chopped.
3. Mix together the chicken, vegetables, egg, garlic, almond flour, oregano and salt in a bowl. Roll into heaping tablespoon-sized balls and flatten slightly to form a nugget.

4. For the coating, place the whisked egg in a small shallow bowl. Mix together the almond flour, oregano and salt in another shallow bowl.
5. Place each nugget in the egg and then the almond flour mixture to coat on all sides. Place on the prepared baking sheet.
6. Bake in the oven for 20 minutes, flipping halfway through.

Storage: Store the nuggets in an airtight container in the fridge for up to 2 days or in the freezer for up to 1 month.

Lunchbox/Picnic: Store the chicken nuggets in an insulated lunch box or cooler with an ice pack.

Cucumber Avocado Gazpacho

Serves: 3
Prep time: 5 minutes
Cook time: 0 minutes

Ingredients:

- 2 avocados
- 1 large cucumber, peeled
- 1 ¼ cups filtered water
- ¼ cup homemade yogurt
- ¼ cup fresh basil
- 2 cloves garlic
- 2 Tbsp. lime juice
- ½ tsp. mineral salt
- 1 pinch cayenne pepper (optional)
- Olive oil (for serving)
- Mineral salt and pepper (for serving)

Directions:

1. Combine all of the ingredients in a blender and blend until smooth. If the soup is too thick, add additional water until it reaches a consistency you like. Add salt and pepper to taste.
2. Store in the fridge and serve chilled topped with a drizzle of olive oil.

Storage: Store the soup in an airtight container in the fridge for up to 3 days. Simply stir before serving.

Lunchbox/Picnic: Keep it fresh and chilled by placing a sealed sandwich bag full of ice cubes into the soup. Remove the ice bag before eating.

Baby Food: This soup makes great baby food with the salt and cayenne pepper omitted. Omit the yogurt if avoiding dairy.

Lemony Lentil Spinach Salad

Serves: 4
Prep time: 10 minutes
Cook time: 0 minutes

Ingredients:

- 2 cups green lentils, cooked
- 3 cups baby spinach, chopped
- 2 large carrots, grated
- ½ cup raw walnuts, chopped
- ½ cup parsley, chopped
- ⅓ cup lemon juice
- ⅓ cup olive oil
- 2 cloves garlic, minced
- ½ tsp. mineral salt

Directions:

1. In a large bowl, combine the lentils, spinach, carrots, walnuts, and parsley .
2. In a small bowl, whisk together the lemon juice, olive oil, garlic and salt.
3. Add the dressing to the salad and toss to combine.

Storage: Store any leftover salad in an airtight container in the fridge for up to 2 days.

Lunchbox/Picnic: Perfect to bring on a picnic or pack for lunch. This will keep at room temperature for up to 2 hours or, alternatively, store in an insulated bag with an ice pack.

Avocado Salmon Salad

Serves: 4
Prep time: 15 minutes
Cook time: 0 minutes

Ingredients:

- 2 ripe avocados, mashed
- 2 (3 ounce) wild caught salmon filets, cooked, and flaked
- 1 large carrot, peeled and shredded
- 2 cups spinach, finely chopped
- 2 Tbsp. lemon juice
- ½ tsp. mineral salt

Directions:

1. In a large bowl, add the avocado and mash with a fork. Add the remaining ingredients and mix to combine.
2. Serve on a slice of GAPS bread or on top of greens.

Storage: Store any leftover salad in an airtight container in the fridge for up to 2 days.

Baby food: This salad is great for babies, if you make sure to chop everything very small, when age appropriate.

Lunchbox/Picnic: Perfect to bring on a picnic or pack for lunch. Store in an insulated bag with an ice pack.

Chicken Taco Salad

Serves: 4
Prep time: 15 minutes
Cook time: 0 minutes

Ingredients:

- ¼ cup cold-pressed olive oil
- 2 Tbsp. lime juice
- 1 tsp. mineral salt
- 1 tsp. garlic powder
- 1 tsp. ground cumin
- ½ tsp. onion powder
- ½ tsp. paprika
- ¼ tsp. oregano
- 1 lb. chicken, cooked and shredded
- 4 cups romaine lettuce, chopped
- 1 tomato, chopped
- 1 red bell pepper, chopped
- ½ cup cilantro, chopped
- 1 avocado, sliced

Directions:

1. In a large bowl, whisk together the olive oil, lime juice, salt and spices.
2. Add the remaining ingredients and toss to combine.
3. Serve topped with sliced avocado.

Storage: Store any leftover salad in an airtight container in the fridge for up to 2 days.

Baby food: Serve chicken and avocado sliced separately.

Lunchbox/Picnic: Perfect salad to bring on a picnic or pack for lunch. Store in an insulated bag with an ice pack.

African Chicken Peanut Stew

Serves: 6
Prep time: 15 minutes
Cook time: 40 minutes

Ingredients:

- 2 Tbsp. homemade ghee
- 1 onion, chopped
- 1 tsp. mineral salt
- 1 red bell pepper, chopped
- 2 cups butternut squash, peeled and cut into bite-sized cubes
- 2 cloves garlic
- 1 tsp. ground turmeric
- 1 Tbsp. fresh ginger, minced
- ½ tsp. ground coriander
- ½ tsp. ground cinnamon
- 2 cups homemade tomato purée
- 2 cups homemade coconut milk
- 1 cup homemade meat stock
- 1 ½ lb. chicken thighs, boneless and skinless
- ½ cup peanut butter
- 2 cups kale, chopped
- Fresh cilantro (for topping)
- Chopped peanuts (for topping)
- Lime wedges (for topping)

Directions:

1. In a large skillet, melt the ghee over a medium heat. Add the onion and salt and cook until softened, for about 5 minutes. Add the red bell pepper, butternut squash, garlic, turmeric, ginger, coriander and cinnamon. Cook for 30 seconds, stirring constantly.
2. Add the tomato purée, coconut milk, stock and chicken. Simmer, uncovered, for 30 minutes, or until the chicken is cooked through.

95

3. Transfer the chicken to a cutting board and shred the meat, then return to the pot. Stir in the peanut butter and kale and simmer for an additional 2 minutes.
4. Serve topped with cilantro, peanuts and a lime wedge.

Storage: Store any leftover stew in an airtight container in the fridge for up to 2 days.

Baby food: Cook the chicken and squash separately for a nut- and spice-free dinner.

Lunchbox/Picnic: Pack this stew in an airtight container on ice in an insulated lunchbox. Reheat before eating.

Egg Salad Stuffed Peppers

Serves: 2
Prep time: 10 minutes
Cook time: 0 minutes

Ingredients:

- ½ avocado
- 4 organic pasture-raised eggs, hard boiled
- 1 cup spinach, chopped
- 2 stalks celery, chopped
- 2 Tbsp. homemade yogurt
- 2 tsp. lemon juice
- 1 tsp. cold pressed olive oil
- ¼ tsp. mineral salt
- ¼ tsp. black pepper, freshly ground
- 1 large red bell pepper

Directions:

1. In a small bowl, add the avocado and eggs and use a fork to mash them together.
2. Add the spinach, celery, yogurt, lemon juice, olive oil, salt and pepper. Mix thoroughly to combine.
3. Remove the stem from the bell pepper. Cut in half lengthwise and remove the seeds. Fill each pepper with the egg salad and enjoy!

Storage: Store any leftovers in an airtight container in the fridge for up to 3 days.

Baby Food: Mash avocado and egg together separately for perfect baby food.

Lunchbox/Picnic: Pack the egg salad and bell peppers separately in airtight containers on ice in an insulated lunchbox or cooler. When you are ready to eat it, scoop the egg salad into each bell pepper.

Curried Coconut Beef Soup

Serves: 4
Prep time: 10 minutes
Cook time: 30 minutes

Ingredients:

- 1 Tbsp. coconut oil
- 2 carrots, chopped
- 1 onion, chopped
- ½ tsp. mineral salt
- 2 Tbsp. curry powder (additive-free)
- 3 cups homemade meat stock
- 2 ½ cups homemade coconut milk
- 1 lb. beef stew meat, cut into bite-sized pieces
- 3 cups kale, chopped
- 1 Tbsp. lime juice

Directions:

1. In large pot, heat the oil over a medium heat. Add the carrots, onion and salt and cook until softened, for about 5 minutes. Add the curry powder and cook for 30 seconds.
2. Add the stock, coconut milk and beef. Bring to a boil, then reduce heat to low and simmer for 25 minutes or until the beef is cooked.
3. Stir in the kale and lime juice. Taste and add more salt if needed.

Storage: Store any leftovers in an airtight container in the fridge for up to 3 days.

Baby Food: Cook the beef separately and cut into strips for your baby with any leftover cooked vegetables.

Eggplant Pizza Casserole

Serves: 4
Prep time: 15 minutes
Cook time: 45 minutes

Ingredients:

- 1 eggplant, sliced into 2" wide strips.
- 1 lb. ground pork
- 2 cups gouda, shredded
- ½ cup Parmesan cheese, grated
- 2 cups tomato purée, homemade
- ½ cup basil, chopped
- ½ tsp. mineral salt
- ¼ tsp. cracked black pepper

Directions:

1. Preheat the oven to 400°F. Lightly grease a casserole dish.
2. Add half a cup of tomato purée to the casserole dish and spread it around. Place the eggplant slices on top to cover the bottom and sprinkle with salt. Put the ground pork on top in chunks. Sprinkle with more salt and some pepper.
3. Top with the remaining tomato purée. Sprinkle the gouda and Parmesan cheese on top.
4. Bake in the oven for 45 minutes, or until the pork is cooked through and the cheese is bubbling.
5. Allow it to cool for a few minutes before serving it topped with fresh basil.

Storage: Store any leftovers in an airtight container in the fridge for up to 2 days.

Baby Food: Add eggplant, pork and tomato purée to a separate baking dish to cook separately if avoiding dairy.

Lunchbox/Picnic: Pack this in an airtight container on ice in an insulated lunchbox or cooler. Reheat before consuming.

Turkey Pesto Zucchini Roll-Ups

Serves: 2
Prep time: 20 minutes
Cook time: 4 minutes

Ingredients:

- 2 cups fresh basil
- 1 cup cashews
- ½ cup Parmesan cheese, grated (optional)
- 1 clove garlic
- 3 Tbsp. lemon juice
- ½ tsp. mineral salt
- ½ cup cold-pressed olive oil
- 2 large zucchinis, cut into ¼-inch thick slabs
- ½ lb. turkey breast, cooked, sliced and torn into bite-sized pieces
- Coconut oil for cooking

Directions:

1. In a food processor or high-speed blender, add the basil, cashews, Parmesan cheese (if using), garlic, lemon juice and salt. Pulse until everything is finely chopped. With the processor still on, slowly drizzle in the olive oil.
2. In a large skillet, heat the coconut oil over a medium heat. Add the zucchini slabs and cook on each side for 1-2 minutes, to soften. Transfer to a plate or cutting board.
3. To assemble, spread the pesto on top of the zucchini. Next, place strips of turkey on top. Carefully roll up the zucchini for a portable lunch. Repeat with each zucchini slab.

Storage: Store any leftover roll-ups in an airtight container in the fridge for up to 2 days.

Baby Food: Omit the pesto in these roll-ups for a baby-friendly lunch.

Lunchbox/Picnic: Pack these in an airtight container in an insulated lunchbox or cooler for the perfect portable lunch.

DINNER

Turkey with Mashed Cauliflower and Avocado Sauce

Serves: 4
Prep time: 10 minutes
Cook time: 40-50 minutes

Ingredients:

- 2 lb. turkey breast
- 1 large head cauliflower, cut into florets
- ¼ cup homemade coconut milk
- 2 Tbsp. homemade chicken or beef stock
- 1 clove garlic, minced
- ½ cup chives, chopped
- ½ tsp. mineral salt
- ¼ tsp. pepper

For the avocado sauce:

- 2 avocados
- 2 garlic cloves
- 3 Tbsp. lemon juice
- 2 Tbsp. cold pressed olive oil
- ¼ cup fresh basil or cilantro
- Salt and pepper

Directions:

1. In a large pot, bring enough water to a boil to cover the turkey. Add the turkey to the pot and simmer until cooked through, for about 30-40 minutes.
2. Fill a separate pot with 2 inches of water and bring to a simmer. Add the cauliflower and steam, covered, for 10 minutes or until completely cooked through.

3. Drain any water from the cauliflower pot. Add the coconut milk, stock, garlic, chives, salt and pepper and use a masher to mash it all up. If you don't have a masher, add everything to a blender and pulse until smooth.
4. In a blender, add all the sauce ingredients and blend until smooth. If it is too thick, add a splash of water until a good consistency is reached.
5. Serve the turkey breast with the mashed cauliflower and topped with the avocado sauce.

Storage: Store the turkey or avocado sauce in an airtight container in the fridge for up to 2 days. Store the mashed cauliflower in an airtight container in the fridge for up to 5 days.

Baby Food: The mashed cauliflower makes great baby food, whether spoon-fed or doing baby-led weaning.

Chicken and Vegetable White Bean Soup

Serves: 3
Prep time: 10 minutes
Cook time: 25 minutes

Ingredients:

- 2 Tbsp. coconut oil
- 1 onion, chopped
- 2 carrots, chopped
- ½ tsp. mineral salt
- 5 cups homemade chicken or vegetable stock
- 1 lb. chicken breast
- 2 cups white navy beans, soaked and cooked
- 1 cup cauliflower florets
- 1 cup cremini mushrooms, sliced
- 2 cloves garlic, smashed
- 2 cups kale, chopped

Directions:

1. In a large pot, heat the coconut oil over a medium heat. Add the onion, carrots and salt and cook for 5 minutes, stirring occasionally.
2. Add the stock, chicken, beans, cauliflower, mushrooms and garlic. Bring to a boil, then simmer, covered, for 20 minutes or until the chicken is cooked through. Stir in the kale.
3. Remove from the heat and use two forks to shred the chicken. Taste and add more salt or a squeeze of lemon as desired.

Storage: Store any leftovers in an airtight container in the fridge for up to 5 days or in the freezer for up to a month.

Baby Food: Omit the salt and purée some of the soup to turn it into baby food when age appropriate.

Sloppy Joe Stew

Serves: 6
Prep time: 10 minutes
Cook time: 20 minutes

Ingredients:

- 2 Tbsp. coconut oil
- 2 lb. grass-fed ground beef
- 1 onion, chopped
- 2 carrots, chopped
- 3 cloves garlic, chopped
- 1 tsp. mineral salt
- 2 tsp. chili powder, additive-free
- 1 tsp. paprika
- ½ tsp. ground allspice
- 1 red bell pepper, chopped
- 2 cups homemade meat stock
- 4 cups homemade tomato purée
- ⅓ cup raw honey
- 2 Tbsp. apple cider vinegar
- Homemade yogurt (for serving)

Directions:

1. In a large pot, heat the coconut oil over a medium heat. Add the beef and cook to brown, breaking it up with a spoon. Add the onion, carrots, garlic and salt and cook for 5 more minutes.
2. Add the chili powder, paprika, allspice and bell pepper and cook for 30 seconds, stirring often.
3. Add the stock, tomato purée, honey and apple cider vinegar. Bring to a boil, then simmer, covered, for 15 minutes or until the stew thickens a bit.
4. Serve topped with a dollop of homemade yogurt, if desired.

Storage: Store any leftovers in an airtight container in the fridge for up to 3 days or in the freezer for up to a month.

Baby Food: Make separate beef patties and set aside some carrots to cook separately

Chicken and Broccoli Satay

Serves: 4
Prep time: 10 minutes
Cook time: 25 minutes

Ingredients:

For the chicken and broccoli:

- 2 lb. chicken thighs
- 1 head of broccoli, cut into florets
- 2 Tbsp. coconut oil, melted
- ½ tsp. mineral salt
- ¼ tsp. pepper

For the peanut sauce:

- ½ cup peanut butter
- ¼ cup homemade coconut milk
- 1 Tbsp. raw honey
- 1 Tbsp. apple cider vinegar
- 1 Tbsp. ginger root, grated
- 2 tsp. sesame oil
- 3 cloves garlic, minced
- ½ tsp. mineral salt
- Water (to thin)

Directions:

1. Preheat the oven to 375°F. Line a baking sheet with parchment paper. Add the chicken to one half of the baking sheet and the broccoli to the other. Drizzle the chicken and broccoli with coconut oil and sprinkle with salt and pepper.
2. Bake for 20-25 minutes or until the chicken is cooked through.
3. For the peanut sauce, add all of the ingredients into a small pot over a low heat and whisk until smooth. Add 1 tablespoon of water at a time until the sauce reaches a good consistency.

4. Serve the chicken and broccoli drizzled with the peanut sauce.

Storage: Store the chicken and broccoli in an airtight container in the fridge for up to 2 days. Store the peanut sauce in the fridge for up to 5 days.

Baby Food: Steam some extra broccoli and purée it with salt-free, homemade stock.

Parmesan Crusted Chicken and Veggies

Serves: 2
Prep time: 10 minutes
Cook time: 30 minutes

Ingredients:

- 2 organic pasture-raised eggs, whisked
- ½ lb. boneless and skinless chicken thighs
- ½ cup Parmesan cheese
- 2 cups cauliflower florets
- 2 carrots, chopped
- 1 Tbsp. coconut oil, melted
- ¼ tsp. mineral salt

Directions:

1. Preheat the oven to 400°F. Line a baking sheet with parchment paper.
2. Place the cauliflower and carrots on the baking sheet, sprinkle with salt and toss with melted coconut oil. Bake for 10 minutes.
3. Sprinkle the chicken thighs generously with salt. Dip the thighs in the egg wash, then place on the baking sheet and sprinkle generously with the Parmesan cheese.
4. Bake an additional 20 minutes or until the chicken is cooked through.

Storage: Store any leftover chicken and vegetables in an airtight container in the fridge for up to 2 days

Baby Food: Omit the cheese if avoiding dairy.

Taco Cauliflower Rice Skillet

Serves: 4
Prep time: 10 minutes
Cook time: 15 minutes

Ingredients:

- 4 cups cauliflower florets
- 2 Tbsp. coconut oil
- ½ onion, chopped
- 1 lb. ground turkey
- 1 tsp. cumin
- 1 tsp. chili powder
- 1 tsp. dried oregano
- ½ tsp. mineral salt
- 1 cup tomatoes, chopped
- 2 avocados, sliced
- ½ cup fresh cilantro, sliced

Directions:

1. Add the cauliflower to a food processor and pulse until it forms a coarse rice texture.
2. Heat the oil in a large skillet. Add the onion and cook until softened.
3. Add the turkey, spices and salt. Cook, while breaking up the turkey, until browned.
4. Add the cauliflower rice and tomatoes, and cook for 1 minute, stirring occasionally, or until the turkey is cooked through and the cauliflower is softened. If it seems dry or it is sticking, add a few splashes of water to the pan.
5. Serve topped with the avocado and cilantro.

Storage: Store any leftovers in an airtight container in the fridge for up to 2 days.

Baby Food: Form the turkey into patties without the spices and bake in the oven with extra cauliflower florets separately.

Tomato and Pesto Burger

Serves: 4
Prep time: 10 minutes
Cook time: 10 minutes

Ingredients:

- 2 cups fresh basil
- 1 cup cashews
- ½ cup Parmesan cheese, grated (optional)
- 1 clove garlic
- 3 Tbsp. lemon juice
- ½ tsp. mineral salt
- ½ cup cold-pressed olive oil
- 1 lb. grass-fed ground beef
- 1 tsp. mineral salt
- 2 Tbsp. homemade ghee
- 1 tomato, sliced

Directions:

1. In a food processor or blender, add the basil, cashews, Parmesan cheese (if using), garlic, lemon juice and salt. Pulse until everything is finely chopped.
2. With the processor still on, drizzle in the oil to emulsify the pesto and blend until smooth.
3. In a bowl, mix together the ground beef and a quarter cup of the pesto. Set aside the rest of the pesto to put on top. Form the ground beef into 4 burgers.
4. In a large skillet, heat the ghee over a medium heat. Once the ghee is hot, add the burgers to the skillet and cook for 3-5 minutes per side, or until cooked through.
5. Serve the burgers topped with pesto and tomato.

Storage: Store any leftover burgers in an airtight container in the fridge for up to 3 days. Store pesto in an airtight container in the fridge for up to 1 week.

Baby Food: Set aside some of the ground beef and form into separate patties.

Chicken Cutlets with Roasted Carrots

Serves: 4
Prep time: 15 minutes
Cook time: 30 minutes

Ingredients:

- 8 medium carrots
- 2 Tbsp. coconut oil, melted
- ¼ cup homemade ghee, for frying
- 1 lb. organic chicken cutlets or tenders (thinly-sliced, boneless and skinless chicken)
- 2 organic pasture-raised eggs
- 1 cup almond flour
- 2 tsp. mineral salt, divided
- 1 tsp. dried oregano
- Lemon wedges (for serving)

Directions:

1. Preheat the oven to 305°F. Line a baking sheet with parchment paper.
2. Place the carrots on the baking sheet and drizzle with melted coconut oil and 1 tsp. salt.
3. Bake for 20-25 minutes, or until cooked through.
4. In the meantime, whisk together the eggs in a shallow bowl. Combine the almond flour, 1 tsp. salt and oregano in separate shallow bowl.
5. Take a cutlet and coat it in the egg on both sides, then repeat with the almond mixture. Repeat with each cutlet.
6. In a large skillet, melt the ghee over a medium heat. Once hot, place the cutlets in the pan and cook on each side for 2 minutes or until cooked through, being careful not to burn the coating.
7. Serve the cutlets with a lemon wedge and roasted carrots.

Storage: Store any leftover cutlets in an airtight container in the fridge for up to 3 days. Store any leftover carrots in an airtight container in the fridge for up to 3-5 days.

Baby Food: These cutlets and carrots are perfect for your baby, unless avoiding nuts. Omit the salt and cut them into slices as finger food.

Bolognese Zoodles

Serves: 4
Prep time: 5 minutes
Cook time: 30 minutes

Ingredients:

- 3 Tbsp. homemade ghee
- 1 onion, chopped
- 2 carrots, chopped
- 1 tsp. mineral salt
- 2 red bell peppers, chopped
- 1 lb. grass-fed ground beef
- 2 cups homemade tomato purée
- ½ cup basil, chopped
- 4 cups homemade meat stock
- 4 zucchinis, peeled into noodles
- Parmesan cheese, grated (for topping)

Directions:

1. In a large skillet, melt 1 tablespoon of ghee. Add the zucchini noodles and sauté for 2 minutes to soften. Transfer to a bowl.
2. In the same skillet, melt the remaining 2 tablespoons of ghee over a medium heat. Add the onion, carrots and salt and cook until softened.
3. Add the bell peppers, ground beef, tomato purée, basil and stock. Simmer for 20 minutes to let the sauce thicken.
4. Serve on top of the zucchini noodles and top with Parmesan, if desired.

Storage: Store any leftover Bolognese in an airtight container in the fridge for up to 3 days.

Baby Food: This recipe is baby-friendly if you omit the salt. Alternatively, you could form beef patties from some of the ground beef and cook them separately before cutting them up into strips. Omit the Parmesan cheese and ghee if avoiding dairy.

113

Honey Mustard Baked Salmon with Asparagus

Serves: 4
Prep time: 10 minutes
Cook time: 10-12 minutes

Ingredients:

- 1 bunch asparagus, trimmed
- 1 Tbsp. ghee or coconut oil for greasing
- 1 lb. wild-caught salmon
- 1 Tbsp. raw honey
- 1 Tbsp. apple cider vinegar
- 2 tsp. mustard powder
- 1 tsp. garlic powder
- ½ tsp. mineral salt

Directions:

1. Preheat the oven to 325°F. Grease a 9x13 casserole dish with ghee or coconut oil.
2. Add the asparagus to the casserole dish and spread into one layer. Place the salmon on top of the asparagus.
3. In a small bowl, whisk together the honey, vinegar, mustard powder, garlic powder and salt. Spread the paste on top of the salmon. Cover the baking dish with tin foil.
4. Bake for 10-12 minutes, or until the salmon is cooked through.

Storage: Store any leftover salmon in an airtight container for up to 2 days.

Baby Food: Roast a cut of salmon separately without the honey mustard glaze.

SNACKS

Sweet and Salty Roasted Nuts

Serves: 4
Prep time: 10 minutes
Cook time: 10 minutes

Ingredients:

- 1 cup almonds
- 1 cup cashews
- 1 cup pecans
- 1 Tbsp. homemade ghee, melted
- ¼ tsp. mineral salt
- 2 Tbsp. raw honey

Directions:

1. Preheat the oven to 350°F. Line a baking sheet with parchment paper.
2. Place the nuts on the baking sheet. Add the ghee and salt and toss to coat.
3. Bake for 10 minutes, stirring halfway through.
4. Remove from the oven, drizzle with honey and allow to cool.

Storage: Store nuts in an airtight container in a cool, dark place for up to 1 week.

Baby Food: Not suitable for babies. Whole nuts should be avoided until at least 5 years old as they are a choking hazard.

Lunchbox/Picnic: These nuts are the perfect packable snack.

Pumpkin Zucchini Muffins

Makes: 12 muffins
Prep time: 10 minutes
Cook time: 30-40 minutes

Ingredients:

- ½ cup coconut flour
- 1 tsp. cinnamon
- ½ tsp. baking soda
- ¼ tsp. nutmeg
- ¼ tsp. mineral salt
- 1 cup homemade pumpkin purée
- 1 ½ cups zucchini, shredded
- 4 organic pasture-raised eggs
- ¼ cup coconut oil, melted
- 3 Tbsp. honey
- 1 tsp. vanilla extract

Directions:

1. Preheat the oven to 350°F. Line a standard muffin tin with muffin cups.
2. In a large bowl, mix together the coconut flour, cinnamon, baking soda, nutmeg and salt. In a separate bowl, whisk together the pumpkin, zucchini, eggs, coconut oil, honey and vanilla.
3. Pour the wet ingredients into the dry ingredients and mix to combine.
4. Divide the batter evenly into the muffin cups. Bake for 30-40 minutes or until cooked through and golden on top.

Storage: Store any leftovers in an airtight container for up to 5 days or in the freezer for up to a month.

Baby Food: Omit the salt and honey from the recipe and chop the muffins into long strips. These muffins make great finger food for babies, especially if you have taken the baby-led weaning route.

White Bean Basil Hummus

Serves: 4
Prep time: 10 minutes
Cook time: 0 minutes

Ingredients:

- 2 ½ cups white beans, soaked and cooked
- 1 clove garlic
- 2 cups fresh basil
- 2 Tbsp. homemade tahini
- 2 Tbsp. lemon juice
- ½ tsp. mineral salt
- ¼ cup cold-pressed olive oil

Directions:

1. In a food processor or high speed blender, add all of the ingredients and blend until smooth. If it is too thick, add a splash of water.
2. Serve with chopped, fresh vegetables (cucumbers, peppers, carrots or celery).

Storage: Store any leftover hummus in an airtight container in the fridge for up to 5 days.

Baby Food: Purée the white beans with olive oil and lemon to make a baby-friendly version.

Lunchbox/Picnic: Pack in an airtight container in an insulated lunchbox or cooler for the perfect snack.

Pumpkin Pie Hummus

Serves: 4
Prep time: 10 minutes
Cook time: 0 minutes

Ingredients:

- 2 cups white beans, soaked and cooked
- ½ cup homemade pumpkin purée
- 2 Tbsp. almond butter
- 2 Tbsp. cold-pressed olive oil
- 1 Tbsp. raw honey
- 1 tsp. ground cinnamon
- ½ tsp. mineral salt

Directions:

1. In a food processor or high speed blender, add all of the ingredients and blend until smooth. If it is too thick, add a splash of water.
2. Serve with sliced apples for dipping.

Storage: Store any leftover hummus in an airtight container in the fridge for up to 5 days.

Baby Food: Omit the honey, salt and nut butter (if avoiding nuts).

Lunchbox/Picnic: Pack in an airtight container in an insulated lunchbox or cooler for a perfect snack.

Garlic Rosemary Roasted Nuts

Serves: 4
Prep time: 10 minutes
Cook time: 10 minutes

Ingredients:

- 1 cup almonds
- 1 cup cashews
- 1 cup walnuts
- 2 Tbsp. coconut oil, melted
- 1 tsp. garlic powder
- 2 tsp. dried rosemary or 1 Tbsp. fresh rosemary
- ½ tsp. mineral salt

Directions:

1. Preheat the oven to 350°F. Line a baking sheet with parchment paper
2. Add all of the ingredients to the baking sheet and toss to coat.
3. Bake for 10 minutes, tossing halfway through.
4. Allow to cool completely before eating.

Storage: Store any leftover nuts in an airtight container in a cool and dark place for up to 1 week.

Baby Food: Not suitable for babies. Whole nuts should be avoided until at least 5 years old as they are a choking hazard.

Lunchbox/Picnic: Pack in an airtight container for the perfect packable snack.

Orange Pineapple Smoothie

Serves: 1
Prep time: 5 minutes
Cook time: 0 minutes

Ingredients:

- 1 cup orange juice, freshly squeezed
- ½ cup pineapple
- 2 tsp. raw honey

Directions:

1. Add all of the ingredients to a high-speed blender and blend until smooth.
2. Enjoy.

Storage: Store overnight for an easy on-the-go breakfast.

Peanut Butter and Jelly Bars

Makes: 12 bars
Prep time: 10 minutes
Cook time: 0 minutes

Ingredients:

- 1 cup cashews
- 1 cup walnuts
- ½ cup shredded coconut
- ½ cup pitted dates
- ½ cup dried cranberries or cherries (no sugar or sulfur added)
- ¼ cup peanut butter
- 1 tsp. pure vanilla extract
- 1 pinch mineral salt

Directions:

1. In a food processor, add the nuts, dates and dried fruit. Pulse until everything is finely chopped.
2. Add the peanut butter, vanilla extract and salt and pulse again to combine.
3. Press into a glass dish and let chill in the fridge for 30 minutes.
4. Cut into 12 bars.

Storage: Store these bars in airtight container in the fridge for up to 1 week.

Baby Food: These bars are not suitable for babies avoiding nuts

Lunchbox/Picnic: Pack in an airtight container for the perfect packable snack.

Snickerdoodle Snack Balls

Serves: 4 (16 balls)
Prep time: 10 minutes
Cook time: 0 minutes

Ingredients:

- 2 cups cashews
- ½ cup shredded coconut
- 1 cup pitted dates
- 1 Tbsp. ground cinnamon
- 1 Tbsp. coconut oil
- 2 tsp. vanilla extract
- 1 pinch mineral salt

Directions:

1. In a food processor, add all of the ingredients and pulse until it starts to come together and is easily formed into balls. If it is too dry, add a splash of water and pulse again.
2. Roll into bite-sized balls.

Storage: Store these balls in airtight container in the fridge for up to 1 week.

Baby Food: These balls are not suitable for babies avoiding nuts.

Lunchbox/Picnic: Pack in an airtight container for the perfect packable snack.

Eggplant Pizza Bites

Serves: 4
Prep time: 10 minutes
Cook time: 30 minutes

Ingredients:

- 1 large eggplant, cut into ¼ inch circles
- 1 cup homemade tomato purée
- 1 cup Parmesan cheese, grated
- 1 Tbsp. coconut oil

Directions:

1. Preheat the oven to 400°F. Line a baking sheet with parchment paper.
2. Drizzle coconut oil on to the parchment paper and spread it around. Place the eggplant circles on the baking sheet. Spread a spoonful of the tomato purée on top of each eggplant slice. Sprinkle the top with Parmesan cheese.
3. Bake for 30 minutes, or until the eggplant is cooked through and the cheese is bubbling and lightly brown.

Storage: Store these pizza bites in airtight container in the fridge for up to 1 week.

Baby Food: Omit the cheese to make it dairy-free.

Lunchbox/Picnic: Pack in an airtight container for the perfect packable snack.

Pumpkin Cranberry Bars

Makes: 12 bars
Prep time: 10 minutes
Cook time: 30-40minutes

Ingredients:

- ½ cup homemade pumpkin purée
- ¼ cup coconut butter, softened
- ¼ cup almond butter
- ¼ cup raw honey
- 2 organic pasture-raised eggs
- 1 Tbsp. coconut oil, melted
- 1 tsp. pure vanilla extract
- 1 Tbsp. pumpkin pie spice (additive-free)
- ½ tsp. mineral salt
- 1 tsp. baking soda
- ½ cup dried cranberries (no sugar or sulfur added)

Directions:

1. Preheat the oven to 350°F. Grease an 8x8 baking dish with coconut oil.
2. In a bowl, whisk together the pumpkin purée, coconut butter, almond butter, honey, eggs, coconut oil and vanilla extract. Stir in the pumpkin pie spice, salt, baking soda and cranberries.
3. Bake for 30-40 minutes, or until the center is set and the edges are browned.
4. Chill before slicing into bars.

Storage: Store these bars in an airtight container for up to 1 week.

Baby Food: You can substitute another quarter cup of coconut butter for the almond butter if preferred.

Lunchbox/Picnic: Pack in an airtight container for the perfect packable snack.

Cinnamon Coconut Cashew Butter

Makes: 2 ¾ cups
Prep time: 10 minutes
Cook time: 0 minutes

Ingredients:

- 3 cups cashews, roasted
- 1 cup unsweetened shredded coconut
- 1 Tbsp. ground cinnamon
- 1 Tbsp. coconut oil
- 2 tsp. pure vanilla extract
- 1 pinch of mineral salt

Directions:

1. In a food processor, add all of the ingredients and process until smooth, scraping down the sides as needed. This will take a few minutes.
2. Enjoy on a slice of GAPS-friendly bread or with sliced apple.

Storage: Store this nut butter in an airtight container in a cool, dark place for up to 1 week.

Baby Food: You can substitute 2 more cups of shredded coconut for the cashews if preferred. Process the shredded coconut until it forms a smooth butter before adding the other ingredients.

Lunchbox/Picnic: Pack the nut butter in an airtight container to pack in your lunchbox as an easy snack with sliced apple.

Made in the USA
Columbia, SC
01 February 2024